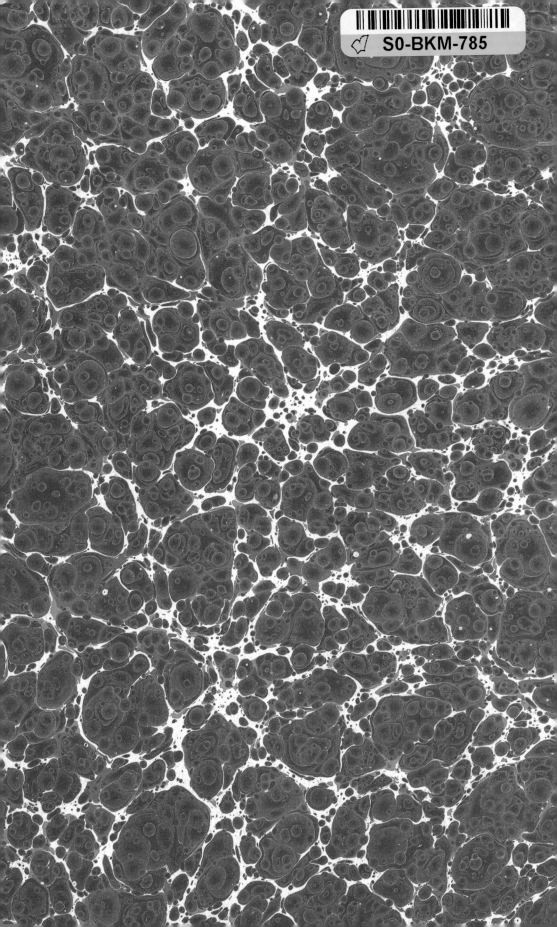

The Bligh Notebook

Captain William Bligh, c. 1803.
Pencil and water-colour drawing by John Smart (1741-1811).
(Courtesy of the National Portrait Gallery, London.)

The Bligh Notebook

'Rough account – Lieutenant Wm Bligh's voyage in the Bounty's Launch from the ship to Tofua & from thence to Timor'

28 April to 14 June 1789

With a draft list of the
BOUNTY *mutineers*

EDITED BY JOHN BACH
**Associate Professor of History,
University of Newcastle**

In two volumes
Volume II: the Transcription

*This volume contains a page-by-page typeset transcription
of Bligh's sailing entries and daily navigation work,
with explanatory notes.
A Preface explains the discovery
and acquisition of the Notebook,
and an Introduction covers the scientific purpose of
H.M.S. Bounty's expedition,
the events of the mutiny, and the voyage of the launch.
A special section for modern navigators
describes Bligh's methods, the tables he used,
and the equipment he worked with.*

This edition specially printed and bound
for Members of
The Book-of-the-Month Club

National Library of Australia
Canberra
1987

National Library of Australia
cataloguing-in-publication entry

Bligh, William, 1754–1817.
The Bligh notebook.
Facsim. ed.
Bibliography.
ISBN 0 642 10426 3.
ISBN 0 642 10427 7 (v.1).
ISBN 0 642 10425 5 (v.2).
1. Voyages and travels. 2. South Pacific Ocean Region—
Description and travel. I. Bach, John, 1923—
II. National Library of Australia.
III. Title.
910'.09164'7

First published 1986 by the National Library of Australia
© 1986 the National Library of Australia
Designed by Adrian Young, MSIAD
Typeset by Deblaere Typesetting Pty Ltd

Published by the National Library of Australia under the
auspices of The Morris West Trust Fund

CONTENTS

Preface   vii

The Illustrations   ix

Editor's Note   xi

Acknowledgments   xiii

Introduction   1

The Transcription   39

The Navigational Calculations   183

Bibliography   211

The List of Mutineers   213

PREFACE

THE BLIGH NOTEBOOK was acquired for the National Library of Australia at auction in London late in 1976. The purchase price of some seventy-three thousand dollars reflected the importance accorded it as an historical document, and was met by a special Commonwealth Government grant. Considerable public interest was aroused by the acquisition.

The notebook was first seen by the public at the Library in January 1977; later that year it was exhibited on loan at several State libraries. Since then it has joined Cook's autograph log of the ENDEAVOUR as one of the treasures of the Library that visitors most often wish to see.

Despite the enormous literature on Bligh and the BOUNTY, the notebook of his great open-boat voyage from Tofua to Timor after the mutiny was virtually unknown until a descendant of the Bligh family offered it for sale in 1976, although a microfilm copy had been available for study in the Mitchell Library, Sydney, since late in 1973.

The particular interest aroused by the notebook focused of course on the question of what new light, if any, it might throw on the character of Lieutenant William Bligh, the subject of partisan authorship ever since the mutiny which gave rise to the voyage. Professor Bach's informed commentary on the transcription now published for the first time reflects his expert knowledge of navigation and his deep understanding of the character of Bligh. In consequence, the reader is enabled to obtain a direct impression of that outstanding seaman from evidence recorded before controversy prejudiced our view of him.

The Bligh Notebook is the first National Library publication to be sponsored by the Morris West Trust Fund, established by the well-known author late in 1983 'for the publication and widest possible dissemination of historic, literary, artistic or other material of national value owned by the National Library.' Other publications of special interest will be similarly funded in the future.

W. M. Horton
Director-General
National Library of Australia

THE ILLUSTRATIONS

T HE ORIGINALS of most of the illustrations used in this book were produced close to the date of the voyage and their existence testifies to
the considerable interest and admiration it aroused at the time. The
fine pencil and water-colour portrait of Bligh *c.* 1803, however, recalls the
first of the two great naval actions in which he served with acknowledged
distinction. The work of English miniaturist John Smart (1741–1811), it is
one of a number of portraits of naval officers he prepared for an engraving
intended to commemorate the battle of Camperdown (11 October 1797). It
became known when exhibited in London in 1937 and was reproduced and
described in the *Illustrated London News* of 13 March that year. It is apparently identical with the portrait frontispiece in the revised edition of George
Mackaness's *Life of Vice Admiral William Bligh,* 1951.

The plan of the BOUNTY's launch, the map showing her track from Tofua
to Timor and the engraving of the boat at sea all appeared in early editions
of the first account of the mutiny, *A Narrative of the Mutiny on board His
Majesty's Ship Bounty; and the subsequent voyage of part of the crew, in the ship's
boat, from Tofoa, one of the Friendly Islands, to Timor, A Dutch Settlement in the
East Indies,* by Lieutenant William Bligh, published by George Nicol,
London, in 1790. Besides the 'Copy of the Draught from which the
BOUNTY's Launch was built', the English edition included charts which
probably provided the basis for the fine map from the edition published in
Berlin in 1791. This map was also to appear in Georg Forster's German
edition of Bligh's *Voyage to the South Sea* in 1793. The *Narrative* was
published in French, by Didot in Paris in 1790, with a map very similar to the
one in the German edition, and by Arrenburg in Rotterdam in the same year.
The frontispiece to the Dutch edition is the engraving showing Bligh and his
men in the boat, faithful as to the launch's two masts, the stormy sea, the
eighteen men on board after Tofua, and the need for constant bailing. All of
these volumes are in the Ferguson Collection in the National Library,
together with other accounts of around the same date.

The well-known representation of 'The Mutineers turning Lieut. Bligh
and part of the Officers and Crew adrift...' is reproduced from the large
coloured engraving by Robert Dodd, published by Evans, London, in 1790.
'Lieut. Bligh and his crew... hospitably received by the Governor of Timor'
is from Peter Paul Benezach's pen-and-wash drawing of 1791, and the view
of Kupang in 1803 reproduces the engraving after Lesueur in the Atlas
volume of Péron's *Voyage de découvertes aux Terres Australes,* the record of
Louis Freycinet's great voyage of 1800–04. All of these originals are in the
Rex Nan Kivell Collection in the National Library.

Bligh's profiles of the north Australian coast, carefully drawn in the log, (volume 2, page 384 of the BOUNTY log in the Mitchell Library), record the sightings tersely mentioned in the notebook on the morning of 29 May 1789. The small sketch of the launch with its two masts on this page is of particular interest.

The photographs of a mariner's steering compass such as Bligh probably used, a Ramsden sextant and the title page of Hamilton Moore's *Practical Navigator*, 1802, were supplied by the National Maritime Museum, Greenwich. The sextant is inscribed 'This sextant was presented to Admiral Sir John Ommaney (then a Midshipman) by Ramsden himself in 1792, being graduated by his hand and afterwards given by Sir John to Capt. Blackwood in 1851.'

The mariner's compass rose reproduced from a National Library copy of Bergen's *Practice and Theory of Navigation and Nautical Astronomy*, 1872, has been included to make clear to the modern reader the now archaic system of compass graduations by 'points', each point being eleven degrees and fifteen minutes, or one-eighth of a quarter of the circle.

The illustrations to this book would have seemed incomplete without some pages from the notebook itself, and the third page bearing Bligh's own testimony to its contents and the pages of 1 June evidencing the presence of the Ramsden sextant on board the launch, previously a matter of some speculation, have therefore been included.

The National Library is pleased to acknowledge the ready assistance of its kindred institutions in assembling these illustrations for this edition of the Bligh Notebook.

EDITOR'S NOTE

THE TRANSFORMATION of Bligh's manuscript notebook into a printed account required several editorial decisions. One of these concerned the abbreviations that abound in the notebook, a natural consequence of the limited space at Bligh's command and the onerous conditions under which he wrote. Some of the abbreviations, such as M^r, Isl^d and even D^o W^r, are conventional and self-evident. Others, however, are made up of part of a word and a terminal letter in a superior position and followed by a stop. The terminal letter is frequently indecipherable, being more of a general symbol indicating an abbreviation than an exact indication of the word involved. It is often impossible to be sure whether Bligh meant, to take an example, 'Easternmost' or 'Easterly', by the abbreviation he used. In such cases, therefore, an editorial decision has been made and the terminal letter of the word thought to have been intended has been employed, but often this has been little more than guesswork.

Bligh's use of capitals presents another problem, since, like so many eighteenth-century writers, he scatters them almost indiscriminately throughout the text. To make matters worse it is not always certain, from the shape of a letter, whether or not a capital is intended, size often being a clearer guide. One cannot say with any conviction that the printed text in fact conveys Bligh's intentions with respect to capitalisation, an admission, however, that was also made by that most distinguished of editors, Professor Beaglehole, with reference to his rendition of Cook's journals.

Punctuation is frequently erratic or missing altogether; an attempt has been made to reproduce it as it stands in the manuscript, including the lavish use of the dash, with or without a stop. Where Bligh has accidentally omitted a word it is, when there is no problem concerning its identity, placed between square brackets.

The reproduction of the information found on the pages ruled in the form of a navigational log required some thought. Because Bligh was using a small book, with limited space on the page, his remarks on the right-hand side are often out of alignment with the hour of the day, marked on the extreme left, to which they refer. Although it would have been possible in most cases to revise the alignment, given the larger space of the printed page, this has not been done, lest some of the sense of pressure and difficulty conveyed by the original be lost.

In the original manuscript the frequent use of pencil is clearly visible, although in many cases the entry has later been gone over in ink. In other instances, however, such as the difference of longitude between the launch and Tofua, which Bligh recorded almost daily during May, the pencilled figures remain untouched. Despite the care taken in reproduction, such pencillings may not be so easily recognisable in the facsimile as in the original. While it has been assumed here that the pencilled entries were all made during the voyage in the launch, it must be remembered that Bligh had the notebook at hand while he was writing his dispatches from the East Indies and his later, published, *Narrative*. It is possible, therefore, that additions or emendations were made at those times; the daily difference of longitude from Tofua could be such a case, but this is only speculation.

Another major decision had to be taken concerning the presentation of the daily calculations scattered throughout the manuscript, since, to a considerable degree, the special value of the notebook lies in its recording of these navigational exercises which are not normally encountered in the finished logs that have found their way into archives and libraries. More than anything else in the notebook these calculations of the day's work, the bearing and distance to a destination and the reduction of sextant readings to the noon latitude, carry a sense of the actual circumstances under which they were performed. It is therefore improper to edit them, for this would involve a tidying process that would be quite artificial. Furthermore, there are occasional obscurities, caused by erasures or over-writing, which would have to be interpreted in an edited version. It is a fundamental rule of historical research, however, that the evidence shall remain undamaged and thus remain available in its original form to later generations of scholars. It was decided, therefore, to photograph all such calculations so that they should be reproduced complete with all their imperfections. As, in addition, they occur in the original in a random order not correlated with the dates to which they refer, it seemed most suitable, for reasons of continuity and appearance, to place them at the end of the main text. Finally, one major principle had to be observed throughout, namely that the transcription volume should be capable of being read satisfactorily without constant reference to the facsimile. Within the limitations of the printed page, therefore, the character of the original has been retained, particularly those aspects which reflect the physical and psychological difficulties of its composition.

ACKNOWLEDGMENTS

M ANY PEOPLE responded to my requests for help and all of them did so immediately and generously, thus making the completion of this edition of the Bligh Notebook possible. I am indebted to them all and I apologise if I have inadvertently omitted a name from the following list.

I must mention first the accurate transcript made of the notebook by Mrs Carmel McInerny, which allowed me to start work with a reliable document that required only minor emendation. I must next thank the librarians who, in their usual manner, put their professional skill and enthusiasm at my disposal. Mrs Baiba Berzins and her staff at the Mitchell Library, Sydney, and Mrs Pam Ray and Miss Barbara Perry of the National Library of Australia are particularly to be thanked for their help with manuscripts and pictures. Essential assistance and guidance were also received from Mr Alec Bolton and Mr Bruce Semler, of the National Library's Publications Branch.

For identification of flora I am indebted to Dr Lawrie Johnson, Director of the National Herbarium of New South Wales, and to Mr Tony Rodd, of the same institution. The late Athel D'Ombrain, the naturalist, assisted with fauna. I thank Captain D. Woods, of Broken Hill Proprietary Limited, and Mr John Quinlan, of the Commonwealth Department of Transport, for the identification of a part of the far north coast of Queensland. Mr Stephen Walters, a leading authority on Bligh, gave valuable advice and information concerning the location of portraits and on the construction of the launch.

While I am most grateful to all the above persons, I must record a particular debt to Mr Alan Stimson, Curator, Navigation, National Maritime Museum, Greenwich, England, and to Mr Vaughan Evans, of Sydney, the leading authority in Australia with respect to eighteenth and nineteenth century maritime technology. Without the help of these two gentlemen I would have found it difficult to cope with the fundamentally important navigational content of the notebook.

J. P. S. Bach
Newcastle
20 May 1985

Page 384 of the second volume of the BOUNTY *log (Bligh's 'fair book' or 'journal', page dimensions, 315 × 200 mm); the notebook entry for 28 May relates. The launch with its two masts is visible at the lower left. (Courtesy of the Mitchell Library, Sydney.)*

INTRODUCTION

T HE NOMINAL subject of this historical introduction is a small leather-
bound and waterstained pocket book, originally the property of
Thomas Hayward, one of the BOUNTY's midshipmen, but appropriated by Bligh to allow him to make navigational calculations and rough notes
of daily events as they happened, while at the same time protecting his valuable official log in a situation which was frequently so wet that he could
scarcely open a book and write. From time to time, when conditions were
more favourable, Bligh wrote up his log and fair journal from the entries in
the notebook, which latter was kept, he tells us, 'in my bosom', under his
jacket and as dry as possible.

The book, according to the catalogue at the time of its sale in 1976 to the
National Library of Australia, remained in the possession of the Bligh family
and its descendants until that date. In the words of that catalogue[1]

> 'With its closely written pages of navigational recordings and reckon-
> ing, rough sketch charts and notes, the Bligh pocketbook provides the
> most complete navigational account yet known of the 3,500 mile
> voyage of the BOUNTY's launch from Tofua to Timor.'

Renewal of the notebook's leather spine has caused the last letters of a few
words to be lost from sight, owing to their having been drawn into the seam.
An occasional word has also been rewritten in an ink that has remained
darker than that originally used. The general form of the contents is simply
described, starting with a brief but continuous narrative of events from the
mutiny on 28 April to noon on 7 May, together with two sketch maps and
some scattered pages of calculations and navigational information. It is not
until 7 May that Bligh started to keep the notebook in the conventional
manner of a log, with five columns on the left of a daily page for the hourly
recording of course, speed and wind conditions, and the remainder of the
page for brief remarks. This more orderly presentation followed upon his
successful manufacture of a log-line two days earlier which, after he had
taught his crew to count seconds accurately, allowed him to measure the
speed of the launch through the water at regular intervals. In order not to
disfigure these entries with arithmetical calculations Bligh set aside a whole
page, sometimes some two or three pages ahead of his current entry, and
used it for the necessary calculations. With rare exceptions the calculations
are dated, making it a simple matter to link them to the relevant log-entry.

This pattern is maintained in the notebook for the periods during which
the launch is at sea. After the arrival on the Australian coast on 28 May the
entries take on the form of a journal, with one or more pages devoted to
descriptions of the environment and the day's events. Throughout the whole

voyage, of course, the official journal was maintained, parts of it often being quite expansive.

From the point of view of the reader the entries in the notebook are often enigmatic and it requires resort to the fair journal to satisfy fully the curiosity thus aroused. In this edition an attempt has been made to overcome this problem by the use of explanatory notes, since the reader may not have immediate access to any of the printed versions of the official log. Bligh's own publications of 1790 and 1792 are, however, more generally available and either would be a useful companion to the notebook.

The ink, probably carried in a pocket writing case, which Bligh used in the notebook has survived remarkably well the ravages of its original exposure to the elements and the more subtle threats of the subsequent 195 years. We know that only Bligh had paper and ink, neither of which he was prepared to share with the BOUNTY's master, Fryer, who was anxious to maintain his own account. He evidently also had a pencil, which he used for several calculations, the occasional note and many of the outlines of the sketch maps. Some of these pencillings, particularly those in the maps, were later inked in. Given the violent motion of the small craft running before the trade winds, made worse by the occasional storm, and the frequent deluges of rain, it is surely a minor miracle that Bligh was able to maintain such a legible account, with so few signs of the inconvenience he was suffering. A comparison of Bligh's writing in the original log, made under more favourable conditions, with that of the notebook, shows how well the latter was kept.[2]

Were this introduction able to be confined to such factual matters as these, or to the technical questions involved in the management and navigation of the launch, while there would still be much of interest to tell, the exercise itself would be relatively simple and straightforward. Such a comfortable passage cannot, however, be granted, since the very presence of eighteen men in a twenty-three-foot open boat on an uncharted sea demands an explanation which immediately confronts us with the great literary and philosophical edifice that in the course of nearly two centuries has been erected upon the events that occurred on the BOUNTY on the morning of 28 April 1789. The mutiny on the BOUNTY has become nothing less than an allegory for our times of the conflict between two opposing concepts of the nature of human society, as relevant today as when it was first fashioned during the bitter verbal clashes between Bligh and those who sought to justify the behaviour of Fletcher Christian.

Although readers of the notebook may be conversant with the main facts of the BOUNTY's voyage and the mutiny there is still an obligation to give some account of them. Originally a trading vessel, of just over ninety feet in length and 215 tons burthen, His Majesty's Armed Transport BOUNTY left England in December 1787 under the command of Lieutenant William Bligh bound for Tahiti, from whence she was to take a cargo of breadfruit

This account was kept
in my bosom as a common
memorandum of our time &
transposed into my fair Journal every day when the weather
would admit with every material circumstance which
passed. — —

                    Wm Wright

          It happened that a Mr.
Hayward had this book with
some signals set down in it wch
appears in two pages & I appropriated the blank leaves to this use.

Page [3] of the notebook.

The Mutineers turning LIEU.t BLIGH and part of the

Lieut. Bligh having completed a collection of six fine Bread fruit plants, set sail from Otaheite the 4th April 1789, & on the 28th before day Ron. Fletcher Christian, with 3 other Mutineers, entered his Cabin, found him out of bed & dragged him bound to the deck, with cut 33 in length, & 9 in breadth & only 9½ deep, was hoisted out, when L.t Bligh & 18 of the Officers & Crew, were forced into it, the Plants that had stocked them, consisted of 16lb of Pork, 160lb of bread, 4 quarts of Rum, 6 bottles of Wine, & 28 gallons of water, with this scanty allowance after endeavouring in vain to procure a greater supply, where in the fruitless attempt one Man was killed by the Natives, they by unprecedented abstinence & resolution, sustained life under divine providence for 41 days, allowing to himself & each man but 1 oz. of bread & 1¼ of a pint of water occasionally a tea spoonfull of Rum & an oz. of Pork, p.r Man, & they, after traversing 3618 miles in this open boat, almost miraculously arrived a composure in his distempered Crew, where they were hospitably treated by the Dutch Governor.——— Vide L.r Bligh's Narrative. Pub.t by order of the Lords Commissioners of the Admiralty.

Pub.d Oct.r 2 1790, by B.B Evans. Poultry, London

Bligh and the others being set adrift on the morning of 28 April 1789, from the colour engraving by Robert Dodd.

...d CREW adrift from His MAJESTY's Ship the Bounty

Engraved by R.Dodd.

To the West India Planters and Merchants,
On whose benevolent representation to Government the expedition for transporting
the valuable Bread Fruit Tree to the British Islands in the West India's was undertaken.
This Print is respectfully inscribed by their most obed.t & very humble Serv.t R.B.Evans.

The launch at sea; frontispiece to the Dutch edition of the Narrative, *1790.*

plants to the West Indies, where it was hoped the fruit would provide a cheap food for the plantation slaves. Bligh was already, at thirty-three, a respected navigator and hydrographer who had sailed on Cook's last voyage to the Pacific as master or navigating officer of the RESOLUTION.

To transport the thousand or so plants during the six-month voyage from Tahiti to the West Indies the BOUNTY had been expensively refitted to resemble a floating greenhouse, a transformation only achieved at the cost of the comfort of the forty-six people scheduled to sail with her. She was nevertheless in first-class seagoing condition when she left England, copper sheathed, well rigged and with ample stores and provisions. It was not the ship that caused the enterprise to fail.

Her complement was unusual in that only one commissioned officer, her commander, was aboard, a fact that contributed significantly to the later trouble. She did not, furthermore, carry a contingent of marines to act as ship's police, a deficiency that also made things easier for the mutineers. Although half of her crew was inexperienced and two-thirds were under thirty years of age, there were nevertheless a few men of greater experience, including Fletcher Christian and two others who had sailed previously with Bligh in a merchant vessel trading to the West Indies, and two men who had been with him on Cook's third voyage, one of whom, the gunner, having in fact been on all three of Cook's voyages of exploration, possessed some first-hand knowledge of the waters around north-eastern Australia and westward to the East Indies.

After a rough passage to the Canary Islands, where she was trimmed, the ship had normal weather until she reached the seas off Tierra del Fuego, at the bottom of South America. On 29 March she rounded Cape Horn, only to encounter three weeks of appalling conditions, during which Bligh and his crew strove valiantly to get clear of the area and out into the Pacific. Finally, storm battered, leaking and with an exhausted crew the ship turned back to run across the southern Atlantic to the Cape of Good Hope, which she reached on 23 May and where urgent repairs were carried out. Thirty-eight days later she sailed towards Tasmania, Van Diemen's Land as it was then called, to anchor on 21 August in Adventure Bay, familiar to Bligh from his visit in 1777. Tahiti was finally reached on 26 October, the ship anchoring in Matavai Bay. Not until 4 April of the next year did she again put to sea, a prolonged stay that played its part in producing the mutiny.

During those five months, while the breadfruit plants were being prepared, the discipline of the crew virtually disappeared and by the time of her departure her people bore little resemblance to a ship's company, a deterioration for which Bligh, as commander, should be held responsible, although he was reluctant to accept such blame.

For twenty-four days before she was taken by the mutineers the BOUNTY moved through the Leeward Islands of the Society Group, touched at the

Cook Islands and on 23 April anchored off Nomuka, one of the Tongan group, previously visited by Cook in 1777. After two days spent purchasing yams and other provisions, together with breadfruit plants to replace some that had died aboard, she again sailed, but not before the theft of several items by the natives had produced a dangerous situation, with a crowd of islanders, some from neighbouring islands, showing great hostility. Bligh for a time held three chiefs aboard his ship as hostages for the return of the stolen goods but at sunset he suddenly relented and sent them ashore. In the evening of the next day a westerly course was set south of the volcanic island of Tofua, on the western edge of the group, and towards Endeavour Strait north of Australia. Just before sunrise on the next day, 28 April, with Tofua some thirty miles to the north-east, the mutineers seized the ship.

A brief account of the seizure given by Bligh in the opening pages of the notebook is followed by a vastly more detailed version set down in the log, probably while ashore at Tofua over the next few days. This second, official account became the source of the despatch later sent to the Admiralty and of the version in Bligh's two published works. The simple entry in the notebook must be seen as the progenitor of a monumental literature on the subject.[3] Starting from Bligh's own explanation, through the evidence at the courts-martial held on the matter, to the present time a host of writers, amateur and academic, has re-examined and reinterpreted, often teleologically, the events of that day.

Many of these commentators, even while observing the canons of historical research, have seemed anxious to justify either Bligh or Christian, and in so seeking have usually confused the distinction between explanation and justification, for there can be no justification of the mutiny, which by definition was a crime that could not and still should not be tolerated by any society claiming to be based on the rule of law, whatever its causes or however sympathetic its observers might be. A mutiny unpunished is an abomination and that is how Bligh saw it.

The reasons why this particular mutiny aroused such great controversy are varied. The fact that the leader was a gentleman, in the terminology of the time, belonging to a reputable and established family which included in the person of Fletcher Christian's brother a Cambridge Professor of Law, has given it a cachet normally denied to the actions of lower deck ruffians, a number of whom were certainly to be found among the mutineers. Professor Christian was faced with something of the same dilemma that confronted John Macarthur before the 'Rum Rebellion' against Bligh's authority as Governor of New South Wales in 1808. The defiance of properly constituted authority, whether defined as mutiny or rebellion, could only be mitigated if it could be proved that the person exercising that authority was unfit to do so.

This is a political sophism with a long history in both Europe and China, and Edward Christian can hardly be blamed for seeking to employ it, the fact of the mutiny being beyond dispute. The consequence of his action, however, was to elevate the crime, then and for future generations, to the status of a symbolical ethical protest, surely an inflated concept with respect to the confused but nevertheless illegal events aboard the BOUNTY.

Other events helped to maintain this trend, including the PANDORA's voyage to the South Seas and her successful recapture of several of the mutineers and their translation from the romantic freedom of the island paradise to the reality of British justice, which added an element both of sentimental horror and high tragedy to an otherwise sordid and reprehensible affair.

If one is able, however, to look at the mutiny not as a mirror of the present but as an event set in its own time and social context, the external events associated with it are of great interest. Most striking of all is the fact that it was not a violent action causing bloodshed, despite the obvious desire of some of its participants to make it one. It was, in fact, a rather slow-moving affair, attended by considerable confusion and indecision, and ending with those cast adrift having acquired all the equipment necessary for their survival, the last result, one would think, that a hardened mutineer would desire. There is no doubt that it was Christian's own highly disturbed state of mind that allowed this to happen, as if he were seeking to atone for the enormity of the crime he had just committed. It is also equally certain that Bligh was determined not to acknowedge any debt to Christian, nor to mention any action of his erstwhile friend that might redound to the latter's credit and arouse public sympathy or even admiration.

There are many descriptions of the mutiny, based largely on the evidence of the court-martial of the mutineers and on two accounts written by those present, that of Fryer, the master, who went with Bligh, and of James Morrison, boatswain's mate, who remained aboard the BOUNTY, to be later captured, condemned to death and finally pardoned. The reader who would know the details of the affair should turn to these accounts, some of which he will find listed in the bibliography. It must be stressed however that before the nineteen men were cast adrift they had managed to obtain water, bread, or ship's biscuit, salted pork, some wine and rum, the carpenter's tool chest, a container of nails, spare sails and cordage, their clothes and hammocks, some of Bligh's papers, including his commission and the ship's log, one of the BOUNTY's steering compasses, a sextant of superior quality, an older quadrant, and two books of nautical and mathematical information necessary for the successful navigation of the launch. Fryer mentions that he had a telescope, which must have been very useful during the passage through the Fiji Islands and later along the Queensland coast. The only serious omission was that of firearms, which the mutineers refused to provide when asked for them. Their absence proved a serious handicap and was a major factor in the death of the quartermaster, John Norton, at the hands of the Tongans of Tofua.

Dimensions.

	F.t in.
Length	23 „ 0
Breadth	6 „ 9
Depth	2 „ 9

8 7 6 5

1 2 3 4 5

Lesueur del.

Kupang about 1803.

Gravé à l'eau-forte par Pillement, terminé par Née

At last, three hours after the mutiny began, the launch, heavily laden and with only six or seven inches of freeboard, was being rowed towards the nearby island of Tofua where, it was doubtless hoped by some of the mutineers, Bligh would be at the mercy of the natives against whom he had taken harsh action only two days before. To Bligh the shock of what had happened to him in such a brief time must have been overwhelming, but the notebook makes no reference to it and we must turn to the journal for its reflections on his situation as he watched the BOUNTY sail out of his life. This journal entry in fact is the start of the still unfinished argument as to the causes of the mutiny. 'I can only conjecture', he wrote[4]

> 'that they have idealy assured themselves of a more happy life
> among the Otaheiteans than they could possibly have in England,
> which joined to some female connections has most likely been the
> leading cause of the whole business.
>
> The women are handsome – mild in their manners and conversation
> – possessed of great sensibility, and have sufficient delicacy to make
> them admired and beloved –'

As those committed to justifying the mutiny in terms of Bligh's own behaviour have often reminded us, his explanation, if correct, effectively exonerated him from any blame and it is indeed beyond dispute, whatever attitude one takes towards Bligh, that he steadfastly refused to accept blame for any of the unfortunate events associated with him.

Much has been written about the character and personality of Bligh and his relationship with Fletcher Christian, a relationship frequently offered as the key to the whole affair of the mutiny, as if the latter were a personal issue between them, the others being mere bystanders. There is no question that Bligh was exceedingly angry with Christian during the three weeks before the mutiny but it is probably not necessary to suggest, as has been done by one reputable author, that this reflected the jealousy of a thwarted homosexual lover. The manifest disgust Bligh revealed for Christian could well have been generated by the latter's having 'gone native' while at Tahiti, which, since he was a respectable and established product of English society, might have seemed far more deplorable than the similar behaviour of the less well-favoured members of the crew. Bligh's own self-denial in the face of the erotic temptations of the island may easily have exacerbated his disapproval of those who were more self-indulgent. This subliminal anger was to become articulate with respect to a number of professional misdemeanours which he could more justifiably condemn, including the well-known failures to wind the chronometer, a heinous offence, and to air the spare suit of sails, both actions which could jeopardise the safe return of the expedition. Once back on the BOUNTY Bligh was able to exact punishment for both the professional and moral misconduct of his crew, particularly that of Christian, whom he ill-treated shamefully.

In examining briefly the general nature of the charges made both against and by Bligh it is necessary to realise that some of the reasons he offered in his own defence are, in fact, unintentional confessions of failure on his part. If his crew deteriorated while at Tahiti it was not the fault of the islanders but of a commander who was not prepared to take effective and timely preventive measures. Naval commanders have always complained of the demoralising effects upon their men of prolonged periods in friendly and comfortable ports. Sydney, for example, the headquarters of the Royal Navy's Australia Station until 1913, was feared by generations of senior officers because of its disastrous influence on the men, who deserted in such numbers that ships were frequently rendered inefficient. Great efforts were made to combat this deterioration of discipline and morale by enforcing regular cruises and sea practices, and by providing organised recreation for the personnel in port. Perhaps Bligh, for all his technical skills, was still too inexperienced in these problems of successful fair weather command.

It is pointless, of course, to pretend to illuminate further the mutiny itself by the acquisition of small snippets of previously unknown information which even if they add a factual detail here and there will never tell us what was happening in the minds of the men who were involved. It is time therefore to turn to our main concern, the voyage of the longboat to Timor and safety.

This is a story that, doubtless because of its brevity when compared to the journal and the subsequent publications, manages not only to stimulate the imagination no less vigorously than any of the speculative theories woven about the mutiny, but also creates a sense of immediacy which allows the reader to observe at first hand the efforts of a skilled seaman to cope with the variety of technical problems now suddenly confronting him. Although Bligh never entirely forgets that what he is writing will one day be used to judge him, the entries in the notebook, made under the pressure of the events they record, have more urgency about them than the later, more calmly written accounts of the same events to be found in the journal. This is particularly evident in references in the notebook to his anxiety and to his occasional lapses of confidence in his ability to save the launch and its occupants. One senses a more fallible man than we are allowed to see in his other accounts.

The account of the voyage from Tofua to Timor, as told in the notebook, needs no embellishment, but a brief outline of its chronology and major events may help the reader to follow it more profitably. After casting off from the BOUNTY Bligh made for Tofua, thirty miles distant, where he hoped to reorganise the launch, obtain fresh provisions and generally prepare for a longer voyage. In this he was disappointed, since the island provided little food and the natives, after an initial show of friendliness, became hostile, partly perhaps as a result of their having knowledge of Bligh's treatment of the chief at Nomuka.

The launch managed to escape late in the afternoon of 3 May, but not before Norton had been killed while trying with great courage to free the grapnel that secured it to the shore, and other members of the crew had been injured by the stones flung by the pursuing Tongans. Realising that he would, being without firearms, suffer the same treatment at any of the islands, Bligh abandoned his plan of sailing south to Tongatapu and encouraged by his men shaped his course to the northwest, towards Fiji and ultimately Timor, 3600 miles distant, where a Dutch settlement existed at Kupang. Since he could have no certain knowledge of the fate of the fleet that sailed for New South Wales a short time before his own departure from England he chose not to sail in that direction, a fortunate decision since the launch may not have survived the more turbulent southern seas.

The long journey began at eight in the evening of 3 May to end in Kupang on 15 June; during its early part the launch passed through the centre of the Fiji group, only twice previously sighted by Europeans, where it was pursued for a time by two large sailing canoes. After Fiji the next sighting was of the group of islands off the northern end of the New Hebrides which today bears the name give to it by Bligh in honour of his patron, Sir Joseph Banks. Here he altered his course more to the west and in due course he reached the Great Barrier Reef in the early hours of the morning, exactly one calendar month after the mutiny.

The events on the six days along the Queensland coast are recorded in the notebook and, as usual, in more detail in the journal. Temporarily refreshed by the diet of oysters and clams and the few beans and berries available on the coast, the eighteen men crossed into the Arafura Sea not by the Endeavour Strait used by Cook, the entrance to which was not identified by Bligh, but by a more difficult passage to the north. A week after leaving Australia, or New Holland as it was called, they saw Timor and, sailing south-west along the coast, finally reached Kupang after forty-two days and 3700 nautical miles in the launch.

The notebook ends at Kupang, but not so the travail of the launch's people. Although hospitably treated in Timor, they had to make their way to Batavia before they could obtain a passage home to England. The voyage through the archipelago, in a small schooner purchased by Bligh, and with the launch in tow, took the same length of time as had the journey from Tonga. Nelson, the botanist, died in Kupang and only seventeen men therefore remained to be found homeward berths. They nevertheless had to split up in Batavia, Bligh with his clerk and servant taking the first available ship, after instructing the others to follow whenever a passage was available, but of the fourteen thus left in Java only nine reached England.

Bligh was formally court-martialled for the loss of his ship, exonerated from blame, and given command of a second and stronger breadfruit expedition to Tahiti. In the meantime the frigate PANDORA was sent to the Pacific, where she captured a number of mutineers, four of whom drowned when the ship was wrecked on the Barrier Reef, where her remains are now being investigated by Australian maritime archaeologists. Of the ten captives who reached England four were exonerated, one was freed on a technicality, two were condemned but later pardoned and only three were hanged.

When Bligh returned from his second and successful breadfruit voyage he found himself for a time the target of attacks from Christian's brother and the family of Heywood, a midshipman of respectable social standing, who was one of those pardoned. He remained on half-pay during this public controversy and it was not until 1795 that he was able to participate in the war against France with his appointment to the command of the CALCUTTA. His war service was distinguished, its high point being the public congratulations bestowed upon him by Lord Nelson for his behaviour at the battle of Copenhagen.

In 1805, while still in command of the WARRIOR, Bligh, now a Fellow of the Royal Society, was offered the governorship of New South Wales through the good offices of Sir Joseph Banks. It was in that colony, while seeking to bring some order to its affairs, that he was the victim of another mutiny, this time called a rebellion, and was deposed from office. Again he was not properly supported, even the commander of the lone ship-of-war in the port retreating behind the legal uncertainty of Bligh's position to avoid taking any decisive action to rescue his superior officer.

After his return to England and the courts-martial resulting from the rebellion, Bligh was promoted to Rear-Admiral in 1811 and to Vice-Admiral in 1814, but he died in 1817 without having hoisted his flag at sea.

We must return to the notebook and to the launch, to the men aboard her, the equipment they possessed and the problems facing them. Although the reader, when confronted in the text with some technical matter, will benefit most from an editorial note provided for the occasion, there are some general practical issues that should be explained before the journey with the launch is undertaken. For convenience these have been dealt with under separate headings.

THE LAUNCH

The launch was the largest of the three boats carried by the BOUNTY, the other two being the jolly-boat and the large cutter, both clinker-built. The launch, or long-boat, said to have been built by the White yard on the Isle of Wight,[5] was 23 feet overall, 6 feet 9 inches in beam and 2 feet 9 inches deep, (7.01 m × 2.01 m × 0.84 m) as shown by the original plan in the National Maritime Museum. Since these vessels were used for taking out cables from the ship they had a strong windlass amidships set on a heavy beam that substantially strengthened them. Long-boats were carvel-built, although the leading authority on the BOUNTY has suggested that her launch may have been built on the double-diagonal system of planking, a system associated with her builders and one that gave great strength to the hull and was virtually leak-proof. A long-boat usually carried one mast and sail for the short cruises often made away from the parent ship, but the BOUNTY's craft had two masts, a foremast well up in the bows and a mainmast amidships, both with lugs or yards from which were set dipping lugsails. The masts and yards are shown clearly in a small sketch made on the Australian coast by Bligh, at the end of his log.[6] The foresail, according to Fryer, was a sail taken from the small cutter and thrown into the launch by the boatswain, who with some others showed great presence of mind in obtaining the essential equipment for a long voyage.

The launch was well designed and performed, as did a recent replica under the same conditions, 'wonderfully well'. Apart from some anxiety about the security of her rudder fastenings, against the possible failure of which he took the precaution of rigging grommets for a steering oar on either quarter, Bligh had confidence in his small vessel. What did threaten her however was her overloaded condition, which allowed the following seas to come aboard over her stern and quarters and thus required constant bailing to be maintained. Bligh's first action after leaving Tofua was to lighten the craft by jettisoning spare clothing and some sails and cordage; a week later he was able to fit a pair of shrouds to each mast, while the carpenter rigged a canvas weather cloth around the hull, which reduced the area open to the sea; the freeboard on the quarters was raised by nailing the stern seats to the gunwale.

The launch, the prerequisite of survival, served them well and one can detect a growing proprietorial tone in Bligh's references to it as the days go past. It may even have been some sense of a bond with it that prompted him to tow the launch from Kupang to Batavia, although it is likely that Admiralty regulations about naval property had more to do with it. The modern reader may have the opportunity of assessing the launch's appearance and qualities from the two replicas that have been built in recent years.

PROVISIONS

While Bligh's handling of the launch under extremely demanding conditions remains a considerable achievement, there were two others aboard, Fryer and Cole, the boatswain, who probably could have done the same task. What neither might have done, however, was to manage the limited resources of food and, to a lesser extent, of water with such foresight and determination that they lasted the entire distance with a little to spare at the end. Fryer, competent though he was, did not possess the confidence or nerve that allowed Bligh to succeed, and the indecision and lapses of concentration from which, if we are to believe Bligh, he suffered might well have led to disaster. Whenever acute despair or ephemeral optimism overcame the crew there was a demand for increased rations and a relaxed regimen; it was Bligh's strength that he was able to resist these pressures.

When cast adrift the launch had aboard 150 pounds of ships biscuits, called bread, sixteen pieces of pork of two pounds each, six quarts of rum, six bottles of wine, twenty-eight gallons of water and four empty water kegs, enough, it was estimated, at a normal rate of consumption to last about five days. Despite all the attempts to obtain additional supplies at Tofua and Bligh's early imposition of rationing, on 3 May, the day of the escape, the supplies were in fact reduced, the pork from thirty-two to twenty pounds, the wine to three bottles and the rum by a quart. A few coconuts and some damaged breadfruit were the only gains from the nearly disastrous visit to the island.

Bligh, with the approval of his men, started rationing the provisions immediately the decision was made to sail for Timor, the original target being an ounce of bread and a quarter of a pint of water daily. The latter was of course far too little and was raised to three quarters of a pint. Before a week was out Bligh, with the aid of a pair of scales made from coconut shells and using musket balls as weights, issued thrice daily 1/24 pound of bread, a total of two ounces, to which was added a small allowance of pork and, while it lasted, coconut milk, with an occasional teaspoonful of rum. A fortnight later still, when approaching the Australian coast, he found that he had left bread enough, at the existing ration, for twenty-nine days. Not being certain he would find Kupang he extended the period to forty-three days by omitting the supper ration. As they closed the land birds became more frequent and boobies, caught by hand, were divided, entrails and all, among the eighteen men. Once ashore inside the reef additions were made to the diet, principally oysters, together with the edible tops of palm trees, a species of fern root and several kinds of berries. With the pork now exhausted these local additions were essential.

When the launch, six days later, entered the Arafura Sea on the last stage of the voyage to Timor, Bligh reverted to his previous rationing scale, augmented for a time by an issue of oysters. Birds again were caught and by 7 June he felt he could safely return to the original thrice-daily issue of bread and still have nineteen days supply left. On 9 June the first fish, a 'dolphin', was caught, although a line had been out for most of the voyage. The only other fish that had been hooked had escaped before it could be landed. When Kupang was reached there still remained food for eleven days, a circumstance in which Bligh took a just pride. The ration, however, was the barest minimum, as the sadly reduced condition of all aboard upon their arrival revealed. Even then they might not have all survived but for the relief obtained during the six days on the Australian coast.

Food was the major problem, but continual saturation and the cramped

quarters also helped to reduce the condition of the crew. In this matter Bligh
was favoured, as he was in navigational matters, by the particular geographical
situation of the launch, since the average temperature of the sea at that time
of the year was around 27 degrees Celsius, considerably higher than that of
the rain that frequently fell. Bligh's instructions to dip the clothing in sea
water and then wring it dry before reassuming it were therefore of considerable benefit.

NAVIGATION

That Bligh was an excellent and experienced navigator had already been
demonstrated elsewhere and there is no question about his competence on
the launch. There has been a tendency however to refer to his navigational
achievement as if it were something in a class by itself, beyond the ability of
a normal professional to perform. This is just not so, the procedures
followed on the launch being straightforward and conventional and far less
demanding than the problems of food rationing, maintenance of morale, and
keeping the launch afloat and efficient. In his log and in other places Bligh
shows a tendency to emphasise the difficulty of the task and the lack of
equipment available to him for its performance. By implication he also
suggests that he is the only person in the boat with the ability to navigate it.
Again this was not the case, Fryer, the master, being qualified for the duty
which, indeed, had been technically his while on the BOUNTY. There is
evidence suggesting that during the voyage to Tahiti Bligh sought to act as
his own navigation officer, a rôle he had performed splendidly with Cook,
with the possible consequence that Fryer felt offended. To say, however,
that Fryer was qualified to navigate the launch is not necessarily to say that
he would have had the determination, patience and optimism that Bligh
brought to the task. It was not the latter's superior navigational knowledge
that brought success but rather his ability to practice consistently, calmly and
accurately the standard procedures available to him, regardless of the
surrounding circumstances.

There is certainly no mystery about the methods employed, as the
notebook, with its daily calculations, proves. It was a simple case of rhumb
line sailing, with plane and mid-latitude problems worked by traverse-tables
in the normal manner. The information needed for these daily calculations
of the launch's position were provided by a Ramsden ten-inch sextant, of
established accuracy,[7] a quadrant of adequate precision,[8] an Adams
compass[9] taken from the BOUNTY's binnacle and a log-line, made up in the
launch a few days after the voyage began and for the use of which the men
had learnt to count accurately in seconds. To provide mathematical,
astronomical and geographical information there were in the launch two
well-known standard printed books, the more important of which was

Ramsden sextant, 1792. (Courtesy of the National Maritime Museum, Greenwich.)

Mariner's steering compass, on pin mounting in a wooden case, c. 1776. (Courtesy of the National Maritime Museum, Greenwich.)

Coming ashore at Kupang, 14 June 1789,
from the pen-and-wash drawing by Benezach, 1791.

Recieved the amount of the present
Drawing this day 7.th 8bre 1791.
P. Benazech.

probably that by Hamilton Moore, a comprehensive manual on navigation and a leading publication in its field, providing by itself all the necessary information.[10]

Like any other method, however, that used by Bligh was only as accurate as the information fed into it, and it was here, in the keeping and recording of the course steered, the meticulous calculations of the distance covered through the water, the accurate observation of the sun's altitude as it crossed the meridian to the north and, more difficult in practice, in the estimation of the effect of currents, leeway and the sea conditions upon the boat's progress, that experience rather than qualifications counted for most. It is a measure of the accuracy of Bligh's performance in these areas that a comparison of his actual position when he reached the coast and his estimate of it reveals a latitude error of two miles and a total longitude error, when converted, of fifty miles after twenty-five days at sea, or a daily average of two miles caused no doubt by the westward-flowing Equatorial current, which he apparently underestimated.

Although Bligh, doubtless for purposes of his own, states distinctly he had only a compass, an old quadrant and an old book of positions, he possessed, as has been shown, all the equipment and information needed for the task. While it is true that the absence of a chronometer rendered impossible the exact determination of longitude, in this he was no worse off than all navigators had been until only a few decades before. The lunar method of finding longitude was not available, there being no nautical almanac on board the launch.

A brief description of Bligh's navigational procedures will allow the numerous references to navigation in the notebook to be read with greater interest. The simplest way of dealing with the problem will be to follow Bligh's actions, in general terms over the twenty-four hours of the ship's day, from noon to noon. Before doing this however it is necessary to mention that he used the method known as plane sailing, which, by ignoring the curvature of the earth and treating small sections of its surface as if they were flat, allows the navigator to frame his data into plane right-angled triangles which can then be solved by simple trigonometry. Bligh was particularly fortunate in that not only was his course close to a westerly direction, thus involving only small daily changes of latitude, but the whole voyage took place less than twenty degrees of latitude south of the Equator, these being precisely the conditions in which plane sailing is most accurate.

The typical navigational day began at noon from a position described in terms of south latitude and east longitude and derived of course from the calculations of the previous day. The courses steered for the next twenty-four hours were known with considerable accuracy, the launch having aboard one of the BOUNTY's compasses. The distance run on each course was measured by obtaining the launch's speed every hour, which when applied to the time spent on each course gave the distance covered. The means of measuring the speed was a log, made up in the launch probably by the carpenter. The normal log was a quadrant-shaped piece of wood, weighted on the rim to stand upright in the water, to which was attached a line marked at regular intervals by a knot. When this was streamed, or hove over the stern, it would remain stationary while the boat sailed away from it, the line running out freely. By counting the number of knots that went past within a specified time, the speed in nautical miles per hour, known as knots, was obtained directly, without further calculation, the proportions of length of line and number of seconds being calculated for that purpose. In Bligh's case the length between knots was probably twenty-five feet and the time fifteen seconds, the figures used by the 'short' log.

At the end of the twenty-four hours all the courses sailed and distance run were resolved into right-angled triangles, of which the distance was the hypotenuse, the vertical side the 'northing' or 'southing' in nautical miles, equal to the change of latitude in minutes of arc, and the horizontal side the distance, in miles, made good towards the west, called 'departure'. By simple addition of the vertical and horizontal distances, totals for each direction covered during the day were obtained. If, at noon, no observation of the sun was possible, the dead-reckoning position for that time was calculated by applying the change of latitude, or distance covered to the north or south, to the latitude of the previous day, and subtracting the difference of longitude, calculated from the departure, from the previous longitude. Because the meridians converge on the surface of the earth as they approach the poles, the actual distance between them decreases in proportion to the cosine of the latitude concerned. Knowing the departure and the mean or average latitude of the day's sailing, Bligh therefore could quickly calculate the difference of longitude represented by the departure.

At noon, however, it was usually possible to observe the altitude of the sun with the sextant. By subtracting the sun's declination, that is, its distance north or south of the equator, which was tabulated in one of the books in his possession, from the complement of the sun's altitude, that is, from the angle obtained by subtracting the altitude from 90 degrees, Bligh found his actual latitude at noon, usually to within two nautical miles. Using the latitude half-way between this observed latitude and that of the previous day, the departure was converted into minutes of longitude; Bligh thus had an actual latitude and a dead-reckoning longitude for his noon position, which was then entered into the log. It must be understood that the longitude was not subject to astronomical verification like the latitude and since it was dependent mainly on the speed of the vessel being correctly estimated, any inaccuracy there, caused perhaps by unknown currents, would produce an error in the longitude.

All the calculations thus involved were basically those of simple

*The notebook entries for 1 June 1789. The reference to the
Ramsden sextant appears in pencil, at top left, and again in ink at the foot.*

Rem.!

High water 3½ flows 5 feet Flood from the
South.d as near as I could observe it. —

At 1 I went to the Top of the Ild saw two
Keys in the N W b N but no Continent
farther than I saw before. —

At 2 Dined sumptuously & at 3 I sailed
for the Keys in the N W b W expecting to
get some turtle. — We are all vastly
recruited by our shellfish dinners. —

Found a kind of Pea that grows on the ground or
Vines species of the Dollacus. —

These oysters grow on the Rocks & are black
& resemble the Mangrove Oyster — They are
very difficult to open or get off the Rocks
reason could get so many

This Ild. is mostly surrounded by Rocks. In
some places Sandy Bay. Fish in the Lagoon —
The one we are on is the West.y Key of Three
that form the Lagoon. — Another Rocky Key
lies to the S W & a small Sandy one near
it. — Toa Tree the leaf of wch is like a Fir
&here & many other Tropical Bushes.
The fine oysters we met with at last Isld are
none here. —

People who are sick attribute their
illness to eating of the Dollacus, but I believe
it is owing to their Berries & to voraciousty

trigonometry as applied to right-angled triangles. Bligh, however, did not have to perform even these elementary calculations for he had at his disposal a set of traverse tables which in effect precomputed all right-angled triangles with a hypotenuse up to 300 miles. Simple inspection of the relevant columns guided by a few equally simple rules gave the answer immediately, whether it was the length of the other two sides when entering with a course and distance, or the total distance run when the departure and change of latitude were known or the minutes of longitude contained in a departure at a particular mean latitude.

This rather lengthy description has been offered in order to show the reader that although great skill and experience were needed to hold a course and observe the altitude of the sun, the last particularly difficult in a small boat, the mathematical calculations needed to deal with the information thus obtained were elementary and second nature to a practising navigator.

The fact that Bligh's course, after he passed the Banks group, lay almost due west benefited him in a further way, since it rendered relatively unimportant the errors that were inevitably gathering around the longitude calculation. He was, in effect, running down a parallel of latitude, a time-honoured procedure, which in due course had to bring him to the coast of New Holland, which his track would cut at a precisely known point, the trend of the coast being almost at right angles to his course. The exact time of the landfall would however not be calculated with certainty, as was shown when the launch reached the Great Barrier Reef nearly a day ahead of the expected time.

Some doubt remains concerning the information Bligh possessed on the actual position of certain essential places to the west of him when he left Tofua. He tended to stress the fact that he had to rely on his memory of Cook's charts of the region, assisted by an old book of latitudes and longitudes, but the calculations of course and distance to such places as Cape York and Timor, contained in the notebook, suggest that several of the positions were to be found in one or other of two books aboard the launch. It is true, of course, that the exact positions given in those works depend on what editions Bligh possessed; furthermore some positions, even in later editions, were not entirely accurate.

There is little doubt, as has already been remarked, that Bligh tried to conceal from public knowledge the extent of his navigational equipment and it is only under the stress of making the actual daily calculations in the notebook that he occasionally leaves evidence of it, with his references to the Ramsden sextant and to Hamilton Moore's book.

Although he had no chronometer aboard which would enable longitude to be determined, Bligh did have, for ordinary log-keeping purposes, a pocket-watch borrowed from Peckover, the gunner. When this stopped on 2 June, near Cape York, he could then be certain only of the times of sunrise and

THE
PRACTICAL NAVIGATOR,

AND

SEAMAN's NEW DAILY ASSISTANT.

BEING

A complete SYSTEM of PRACTICAL NAVIGATION,
Improved, and rendered eaſy to any common Capacity.

THE WHOLE EXEMPLIFIED IN

A JOURNAL kept from LONDON to MADEIRA, and back to ENGLAND.

WHEREIN IS SHEWN,

How to allow for Lee-way, Variation, Heave of the Sea, Set of the Currents, &c. and to correct the dead Reckoning by an Obſervation, in all Caſes.
The Method of Mooring, Unmooring, and Working a Ship in all difficult Caſes at Sea, on a Lee-Shore, or coming into Harbour.
The Manner of Managing the great Guns; of Forming the Line; of an Engagement at Sea; and of Surveying Coaſts and Harbours; with an Explanation of the Sea Terms.
The New Method of finding the Latitude by two Altitudes of the Sun; and of finding the Longitude by the Moon's Diſtance from the Sun or fixed Star.

To which are added,

The Tables of Difference of Latitude and Departure to 300 Miles Diſtance; New Solar Tables; the Table of Natural Sines; a new Table of the Latitude and Longitude of Places, according to the lateſt Obſervations; a Table, ſhewing the Times of the riſing and ſetting of the Sun, Moon, fixed Stars, and Planets; and all other Tables uſeful at Sea.

CONSTRUCTED UPON A NEW PLAN.

By JOHN HAMILTON MOORE,
Teacher of Navigation, &c. No. 104 in the Minories, Tower-Hill, London.

The SEVENTH EDITION,
Carefully corrected, and greatly enlarged by the AUTHOR.

In this Edition are added the Method of finding the LATITUDE by the MOON and PLANETS; and two COPPER PLATES; one ſhewing the SOLAR SYSTEM, the other the TERMS of GEOGRAPHY at one View.

LONDON:

Printed for and Sold by B. LAW, in Ave Maria Lane; G. ROBINSON, Pater-noſter-Row; and the Author, at No. 104, in the Minories, near Tower-Hill.

M,DCC,LXXXII.

Title page of Hamilton Moore's seaman's handbook, 1782. (Courtesy of the National Maritime Museum, Greenwich.)

sunset and, of course, noon, when the sun was due north, but presumably he was experienced enough to interpolate the intermediate divisions by a visual estimate of the sun's changing position, for the log continued to be divided properly into its twenty-four hours.

To follow the chronology of the notebook it is necessary to understand that it is kept in nautical, not civil time. The nautical day started at noon when the sun crossed the meridian, the new day taking the date of the civil day that was due to start twelve hours later, at midnight. For the first twelve hours therefore, referred to as the 'p.m.', the nautical date was one day ahead of the civil date; at midnight, when the nautical day, now half spent, entered its 'a.m.' phase, its date coincided with that of the new civil day just begun and continued to do so for the next twelve hours until noon. In order to avoid confusion all references to the date in this introduction and the annotations refer to the nautical date.

It is time the reader was allowed to turn to the text, but before doing so he or she may wish to know if the notebook makes any significant contribution to the existing knowledge of Bligh and the mutiny and the long-standing controversy concerning them that has been maintained to the present day by both literary and cinematographic means. The notebook, in its references to the sextant and the navigational books on the launch, does offer something new in the way of evidence which will possibly encourage those who have claimed that Bligh's log did not reveal all the events of the voyage and, by implication, might possibly be false with respect to some of the events it does record. Fryer and Morrison both wrote accounts that were critical of Bligh, but in general those defending Bligh have discounted them as being motivated by malice. It is interesting nevertheless that both stated that Bligh had a sextant which, Morrison informs us, was given to him at the last moment by Christian, a deed that must strengthen the belief that Christian was seeking to give his captain every chance of survival, probably as atonement for his own behaviour. Fryer also stated that Bligh had in the launch with him copies of both Hamilton Moore and the *Tables Requisite*.[11] The notebook refers to both as Timor is approached, once again confirming Fryer's truthfulness in the matter. Since Bligh does not mention the sextant or Moore in his log or in his subsequent publications and since, moreover, he says specifically that he had only a compass, an old quadrant and an old book of positions, one faces the question of whether the omission was deliberate, either to avoid showing Christian in a better light or himself in a worse.

The confirmation of two of Fryer's comments must also raise the question of whether his other, harsh criticisms of Bligh are to be taken more seriously than many have done in the past. There can be no certain answer, but in the light of Fryer's later distinguished career his account, probably written in 1790, cannot be ignored, notwithstanding his obvious resentment of Bligh.

Fryer's versions of certain events during the launch voyage will be mentioned when relevant in the annotations.

There are other minor differences between the notebook and the log, but they are of little significance. The great contribution of the work remains the air of immediacy it creates for the reader, with its picture of Bligh writing from the heart in the midst of situations of great danger and unknown outcome. The very restrictions placed upon his writing by the conventions of the log form and the circumstances in which it was being done give to the account a terseness that stimulates the imagination. This evocative brevity and apparent understatement, rather absent from the official log, are charac-teristic of many eighteenth-century nautical accounts. One is reminded, for example, of the manner in which John Hunter describes in his journal the grim fight of the hard-pressed SIRIUS as she clawed off an unknown lee shore during a great gale off south-eastern Tasmania, an event which, by coinci-dence, occurred in the same year as the launch voyage.[12] The notebook, in brief, gives us a rare look at Bligh the seaman, in the full and splendid prac-tice of his profession, and as such he is beyond our criticism.

The notebook itself must of course remain an object for wonder, when one considers what it has been through. The men and their ships have long since been dispersed by the winds of time yet this small manuscript volume survives with its power, as it is put through that most marvellous of all proces-sors, the human imagination, to recreate a world of experience and sensation that transcends both time and space. The written word, of which this notebook is a precious example, is surely one of man's most essential creations without which, even in this age of electronic communication, he would remain a prisoner of an eternal present, deprived of self-image and cultural identity.

Notes

1 *Important Natural History Books Travel and Atlases, including Bligh's Manuscript Account of his Voyage in the* BOUNTY*'s Launch after the Mutiny.* Christies, London, November 24, 1976.

2 See note 1 to page 3 of the transcription for further information on the status of this original log, held by the Mitchell Library, Sydney.

3 This comment is based on the assumption that the entries in the notebook were written before those in the log. This may not be so, however, since it is possible that Bligh did not use the notebook until the launch put to sea on 3 May. We know that he wrote up his log while ashore at Tofua, being engaged, indeed, in that activity only a short time before the natives began their attack. The earliest notebook entries may therefore be a summary of the detailed log entries, rather than the latter being an expansion of the brief remarks in the notebook. Circumstantial evidence supporting this theory comes from the obviously retrospective character of the heading and the account of the acquisition of the notebook given on its third page. On the other hand the calculations for 3 May on page 11 are most certainly a first entry, so perhaps the first direct entry is that for Monday 3 May.

4 *The log of the HMS* BOUNTY, *1787-1789,* facsimile from the copy in the Public Record
office, Genesis Publications 1975, folio 356, Remarks of Thursday, 28th July 1789.

5 For the history of the launch see Stephen Walter's edition of Fryer's *Narrative*
(Genesis, 1979), where the suggestion is also made that she may have been double-
diagonally planked, a method possibly invented by Thomas White, the founder of the
yard.

6 Page 384 of the second volume of the log held in the Mitchell Library and reproduced
here.

7 Jesse Ramsden (1735-1800) was a famous English instrument maker who produced
a device to divide the circle mechanically with such precision that it eclipsed all other
methods to become by 1780 the machine in general use by those making linear and
circular scales of high accuracy. Several of his instruments have survived.

8 The quadrant, described throughout as old, was probably one by Hadley, who
displayed his new precision instrument for the first time in 1731. This instrument,
properly called an octant, was accurate to two minutes and in many cases to one
minute of arc when it was officially tested in 1732. It could measure angles up to 90
degrees; since this was not always enough to measure lunar distances, used for finding
longitude before chronometers were perfected, the sextant, capable of measuring up
to 120 degrees, was accordingly developed. Although the sextant possessed certain
other improvements in accuracy, the quadrant was a perfectly serviceable instrument,
as its single recorded result in the notebook reveals.

9 George Adams (*c.* 1709-1772) was one of the best-known instrument makers in
England; he was succeeded in turn by two sons, George and Dudley.

10 For the titles of these works see note 1 to page 1 of the transcription.

11 James Morrison's *Journal of H.M.S.* BOUNTY *and at Tahiti,* an original manuscript
held by the Mitchell Library, says on page 44 that after Bligh was in the boat he asked
for his sextant and commission. The latter, with his pocket-book and private journal,
was handed down on Christian's orders. Christian, says Morrison, then gave his own
sextant and a copy of the *Daily Assistant* to Bligh, saying 'there Captn. Bligh this is
sufficient for every purpose and you known the sextant to be a good one'. Since Bligh,
in the two notebook references to the sextant, describes it as the Ramsden B, it must
have been his own instrument, which is mentioned on page 4 of the log as one of the
three sextants he was taking with him on the BOUNTY. The *Daily Assistant* mentioned
by Morrison refers to Hamilton Moore; the *Tables Requisite* were brought into the
launch in Midshipmen Hallett's pocket, according to Fryer. George Mackaness states
in his *Life of Vice-Admiral William Bligh,* in a note to page 142 of the 1951 edition, that
'the old book of latitudes and longitudes' mentioned by Bligh in his log entry of 3 May,
was at that time in the Dixson Collection and that it contained Bligh's calculations.
Mackaness was probably referring to the volume now in the Dixson Library, State
Library of New South Wales, described as 'Captain Bligh's Private Log of the
BOUNTY, etc.', which is in fact a bound collection of extracts from contemporary navigation manuals, on several of which, and particularly those dealing with the double
altitude method of finding latitude, Bligh made detailed technical comments. The
book, even if it accompanied Bligh aboard the launch among the ship's papers rescued
by Samuel, his clerk, was certainly not used for navigational purposes. We are indebted
to Bruce Semler and Diana Rhodes, Dixson Librarian, for the above information.

12 This was on 21 April 1789.

THE TRANSCRIPTION

The gaps in the sequence of the original pages of the notebook, numbered here in square brackets at the foot of each page transcribed, are accounted for by the transfer to the navigational notes at the back of those pages of calculations relevant to them. Where part only of an original page has been transferred for the same reason, this is noted in the appropriate place.

1 The first six positions are all in the New Hebrides and were obtained from
   Hamilton Moore's *The Practical Navigator and Seaman's New Daily Assistant,*
   1782 or 1784 edition. The last position, for south-west Timor, is from *The
   Tables Requisite to be used with the Nautical Ephemeris for finding the Latitude
   and Longitude at Sea.* The Second Edition Corrected and Improved. London
   MDCCLXXXI (1781). The actual longitude of Cape Cumberland is 166°38'E.

2 These figures, pencilled in an inverted position in the original, at noon,
   10 May 1789, include the corrections for the sextant reading of the sun's lower
   limb (the lower edge), the zenith distance, the declination and finally
   the latitude.

St Bartholomew 15.42S – 167.17E
C. Cumberland 14.39 – 166.47
C. Lisburne 15.41 – 166.57
C. Queros 14.56 – 167.20
Tanna }
Resolution Port } 19.33 – 169.41
Table Isl.^d 15.38 – 167.07

Timor S.W. 10.23S – 123.59[1]

$$56.53[2]$$
$$-\ 4$$
$$56\ 49$$
$$13$$
$$57\ 02$$
$$32\ 58$$
$$17\ 41$$
$$15\ 17$$

[1]

1 A reference to the official log of the BOUNTY which he had managed to rescue. It is the original from which the official Admiralty version was later probably copied. It has generally been thought that the two-volume log in the Mitchell Library, Sydney, is in fact this original work, but Professor Henderson in 1931 suggested that it is really an exact copy, in Bligh's own hand until August 1789, of the log kept aboard the launch, which may have suffered considerable damage from exposure. A comparison of the Admiralty version and the Mitchell Library's reveals many, if minor, discrepancies; page 4 of the former carries details of Bligh's navigational plans for the voyage that are missing from the second. The log is normally kept in two daily sections, one a tabulated page containing navigational data and brief remarks, the other an expanded and more detailed account of the matters mentioned in the remarks. Here the former will be called the log, the second the journal, whenever a reference is made to either section. (This matter is also noted by Stephen Walters in his edition of Fryer's *Narrative*.)

2 Thomas Hayward, midshipman. The signals information may have been that used by the BOUNTY. Hayward, together with John Hallet, the other midshipman in the launch, was to return in the PANDORA as a lieutenant, to help in the search for the mutineers.

1 Tofoa, properly Tofua, a 1660-foot-high volcanic island on the western fringe of the Tonga Group, sighted by Tasman in February 1643.

2 A league is three nautical miles.

This account was kept in my bosom as a common memorandum of our time & transposed into my fair Journal[1] every day when the Weather would admit with every material circumstance which passed. –

Wm Bligh

It happened that a M.[r] Hayward[2] had this Book with some Signals set down in it w.[ch] appear in two Pages & I appropriated the blank leaves to this use.

[3]

Rough account – Lieutenant Wm Bligh's Voyage in the Bounty's Launch from the Ship to Tofoa[1] and from thence to Timor.

28 April 1789

Just before Sun Rise the People Mutinied seized me while asleep in my Cabbin tied my Hands behind my back – carried me on Deck in my Shirt – Put 18 of the Crew into the Launch & me after them and set us a drift – Tofoa bearing NE 10 leag.[s][2] – Ship steered to the WNW. – Four cutlasses were thrown into the Boat. –

[5]

1 Morrison's journal states that 25 or 26 pieces of pork of four pounds each were handed to the boat as it lay astern on the orders of Christian, together with two gourds of water.

2 The loose sheets placed inside the notebook and reproduced in this edition contain the names and descriptions of these men, set down by Bligh. This list is probably the original of the various later versions that appeared in the log and in Bligh's publications, although the wording varies in minor details.

3 A 'gill' or 'jill' is a quarter pint. Bligh has generally preferred to spell it according to the latter, older, usage, but the modern form has been used throughout the transcription. 'Grog' was rum diluted with water, a practice introduced in 1740 by Admiral Vernon in order to reduce drunkenness caused by the daily ration of neat rum. Vernon wore a boat cloak made from grogram and was thus known as 'old Grogram', from which 'grog' is derived.

1 Another reference to the log and journal.

The Provisions were 150lbs of Bread 16 pieces Pork 6 Quarts of Rum 6 bottles of wine 28 Gall[s] of Water and 4 Empty Breakers – The Pork was in 2lb pieces.[1] – We were very deep & rowed towards Tofoa – 25 Men remained on board with Christian.[2] –

29 April
At Dark got to the Island – could not land – served 2 gills of Grog[3] to each person – In the morning landed with difficulty, in search of Provisions – served a Morsel of

[6]

Bread & Gill of Wine to each Person for Dinner. –

Thurd[y] 30 April 1789
Hard Gales. – At Night served a Cocoa Nut to each Man & slept again in the Boat. – dared not venture to sea – At Dawn of Day served a Morsel of Bread & a Spoonful of Rum to each Person landed in search of Provisions. At Noon wrote up all my transactions in my fair Book[1]

Friday 1 May 1789
Had no success in Provisions. at Night supped on a Plantain & a Gill of Grog – At Dawn of day sent Party away again.

[7]

1 Omitted from the text but obviously intended.

2 The escape from the Tongans was a near thing; it is dramatically narrated
   in the journal. The injuries were caused by stones thrown with force and
   accuracy by the natives, whom Bligh finally distracted by casting overboard
   articles of clothing which his pursuers stopped to retrieve. John Norton,
   quartermaster, was killed while with great bravery he was engaged in freeing
   the stern line which tethered the launch to the shore. His was the only
   death during the launch's voyage.

1 The launch carried two masts, a foremast and a mainmast, with a
   dipping lugsail on each. The foresail has here been reefed, or reduced in area,
   by means of short lines attached to the quadrilateral sail in a row parallel with
   its foot or bottom edge. In simple terms the foot of the sail is bundled up and
   secured by these lines, which are on both sides of the sail. The normal lugsail
   had two such bands of reefing lines (technically, in the case of an eighteenth-
   century lugsail, called reef hanks, although today these would be indistin-
   guishable from reef points; the difference lay in the type of cordage employed),
   and when the sail was gathered up to the higher set it was said to be 'close-
   reefed'. For precise details of a late eighteenth-century lugsail see David
   Steel, *The Art of Sail Making as practised in the Royal Navy*, etc., London, 1796.
   I am indebted to Vaughan Evans, Esq., for this information.

2 'mere', in this eighteenth-century usage, means 'sheer, absolute, downright'.

Saturday 2 May 1789

Stormy W.ʳ Wind ESE – Natives came about us endeavoured to [get]¹
Cocoa Nutts & Plantains – could get no water but 5 pints first trip 3
Gallons afterwards – Natives became hostile – At Noon served a Cocoa
Nutt & Breadfruit to each Person for dinner which we eat under great
apprehension of the Natives – Copied in my Journal

Sunday 3 May

Fresh Gales ESE to NE The Natives in great number prepared to attack
us – I ordered all the People & what we had into the Boat – When in, I
followed & the Natives began their attack Killed Poor Norton – followed
us in Cannoes – maimed us very much – rowed out to Sea –²

[8]

Sunday cont.ᵈ

and after supplication from People at 8 at Night bore away for Timor
after prayers, agreeing to live on a Gill of Water & morsel of Bread our
Stock of Provisions about 150 lbs Bread 28 gall.ˢ Water 20 lbs Pork 3
Bottles of Wine & 5 Quts Rum The difference from our 1st quantity
being owing to loss – a few Coconutts & some Breadfruit were in the
Boat but the latter useless. – divided into 2 watches & set a reefed lug
foresail¹ – at 8 am it blew a mere² storm & were in very eminant Danger
– always bailing & in a horrible situation. served a teaspoonful of Rum
to each Person for we were very wet & Cold – at Noon lat.ᵈ 19° 27′S
183.52 E

Monday 4 May

D.º W.ʳ & distresses great & in the greatest danger of foundering Served
a teaspoonful of Rum

[9]

1 This was Yangasa Levu at the southern end of the Lau Group, which is the
   windward or eastern fringe of Fiji. The island is 390 feet in height.

2 The designations of the seventeen men mentioned here, from left to right,
   were Master, Boatswain, Gunner, Carpenter, Master's Mate, Midshipman,
   Quarter Master's Mate, Sailmaker, Quarter Master, Boy, Midshipman,
   Clerk, Acting Surgeon, Botanist, Cook, Butcher, Cook. (From Bligh's
   A Voyage to the South Sea London, 1792.)

3 Lamb's Christian name was Robert, the initial given here appears to be
   an error.

1 Yangasa Levu.

Monday 4 May cont.^d

Saw land a small Isl.^d mod height¹ It was now Noon great difficulty I could observe the Suns alt.^d Lat.^d in 18° 58' S 182.16 E – Divided 5 Small Coco Nutts for our Dinner Every one was satisfied. – Our three Watches to be²

Mr Fryer	Mr Cole	Mr Peckover
Purcel	Elphinstone	Hayward
Simpson	Lebogue	Linkletter
Tinkler	Hallet	Samuels
Ledward	Nelson	Hall
Jn Lamb³		Jno Smith

[10]

Disc.^d a small Flat Isl.^d of a small height at Noon WSW 4 or 5 leagues¹

[The calculations which form the rest of the original material on this page will be found at the back of the book, with the navigational notes for 3 and 4 May.]

[11]

1 As numbered on the sketch map these islands are (1) Namuka, (2)
  Navutuira, (3) Yuvutha, (4) Navutuloma (5) a high rock and, close to the rock,
  (6) Yangasa Levu. The island to the north, shown in the sketch with two small
  keys close by, is Mothe, and that to the west of it is Komo. This sketch must
  be the earliest version of the chart sent to Sir Joseph Banks, now in the
  Mitchell Library. It is reproduced in Henderson, *The Discoverers of the Fiji
  Islands,* facing p. 130. In the original text, pencilled numbers 1-5 appear above
  the bearings of the five islands last referred to, correlating with numbers 1-5
  on the sketch map. Also, S¼W is S1W in the original; it has been corrected
  here to read as was obviously intended.

2 The longitude is that calculated for Mothe. Its true longitude is 178°30'W,
  or 181°30'E, so Bligh placed it 29 minutes too far east. Since he started from
  Tofua with an easterly longitude error of 25 minutes, he has lost four minutes
  of longitude since Tofua. Bligh states in both notebook and log that the two
  keys are north-east of Mothe, whereas they are to the south-east.

5th May Tuesd.ʸ PM

Soon after Noon saw five Isl.ᵈˢ countg the first seen to the WSW – A large Isl.ᵈ to NW & one to the WNW – At 10 after 3 an other Isl.ᵈ making in all 8 – South Isl.ᵈ bore South. The North Isl.ᵈ NWbN next NWbW½W the next WSW next SSW next SbW – next S½W next S¼W a Rock close to the South Isl.ᵈ¹ –

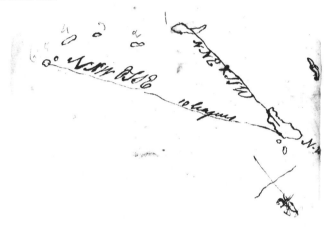

[The Windward Islands of Fiji.]

At 4°.34′ North Isl.ᵈ true North 5 or 6 leagues

NWbW¼W18 –   9:3 –   15.4 = 17
            16   182 . 16
            ___   _____
            25   181 . 59E: North Isl.ᵈ²
           18.58
           _____
           18.33

[12]

1 This is the first of the pages in the notebook containing Hayward's signal entries. Bligh wrote his note along the length of the page.

1 Komo and Olarua, 270 and 250 feet high.

2 In fainter ink than the surrounding text and figures.

3 See the explanation of the log-line in the Introduction.

Signals for Boats[1]
Sent to Discover Anchorage
On Finding bottom to be denoted in the following Manner
1ˢᵗ : *5 fathoms a blue flag.*
2ᵈ. : *10 fathoms a White flag.*
3ᵈ. : *15 fathoms a Red flag.*
4ᵗʰ : *20 fathoms a White and Red flag both held up Together*
5ᵗʰ. : *For every fathom between 5 and* 10 – 10 *and* 15 – 15 *and* 20 *fathoms the flag to be lowered and held up, first making the particular signal distinctly; holding it up one Minute, and the repeaters a Quarter of a Minute between Each.*
6ᵗʰ. : *30 fathoms and upwards a White, and a Blue flag and for every fathom up to* 40, *the White flag to be lowered and held up.*
7ᵗʰ. : *A good harbour or safe Anchorage the three flags to be hoisted together.*
8ᵗʰ : *On discovering Danger, it is to be denoted by firing shotts, and that is to be Continued untill you*

This was part of our Signel Book wᶜʰ. was in Mʳ. Haywards Pocket & served me to make my occurrences in

[13]

At 5 PM saw two more Islᵈˢ to the Westward – They are all of a tolerable height and woody – The northernmost is the highest & has two small Islᵈˢ. off its NE End – At Sun Set North Islᵈ. NNE 5 leagˢ. & the West Islᵈ. in sight NW½W 8 leagˢ.[1] –
D to Sunset[2] Marked a log line and taught the Men to count seconds[3]

[The calculations which form the rest of the original material on this page will be found with the navigational notes for 5 May.]

[14]

1 The second page containing Hayward's entries (struck through in
   the original).

1 Ngau, 2345 feet high, and Nairai, 1104 feet high and much smaller
   than Ngau.

2 Henderson says Bligh actually saw Ngau, the higher of the two islands, and not
   Nairai, as implied by the text.

3 These five islands, in the order mentioned, were Mbatiki, Wakaya,
   Ovalau, Makongai and Koro. Their heights range from Wakaya's 595 feet to
   Ovalau's 353 feet. See pages [17] and [23] for Bligh's sketch maps.

4 The word 'considerable', also used in the journal, has been struck out and the
   word 'tolerable' written above it.

you observe the Ship takes proper means to get Clear of it.[1]

9th : *No boat is ever to go from the Ship without a grapnell, a Musquet, a Cutlass and a Proper Quantity of Ammunition for Each Man, with water and Provisions for that Day.*

10th. : *No more than one man is to Quit the boat at a time in any place where there may be Indians, and if any are discovered, no Man is to Quit the Boat*

11th : *The Officer who Commands the boat is to make himself acquainted with the General soundings of the Place he is examining, and not to lose time in sounding too minutely, but to proceed back to the ship with all dispatch, that being of sufficient for her General Conduct, and if any more is required, a Boat will be kept ahead*

12th : *A Jack at the Main top Gallant Mast head is a Signal for the boats away to repair on board, and will be made with, or without, Guns, as circumstances may make it Necessary.*

[15]

6th May PM at [h]5 3/4 saw two large Isld[s] and very high each of them perhaps 20 leag[s] or 30 in circumference – One bore WbS about 7 leag[s] & the other NWbN about 8 or 9[1] – very hazy & moderate breezes – ENE Steered NbW to Wind of the North[n] one & bore away at 10[h] NW. at 3 WNW – at 6AM NWbW Saw the Isl[d] past last night[2] bearg SSE 10 leg[s] and 5 others a small one SbW 7 leag[s] a little larger one SWbS 1/2 S 6 leg[s] a very large one SW 10 leag[s] – Another middle size West 5 leag[s] and another NE 1/2 E 7 or 8 leag[s][3] past between those two last steering NWbN – These in general are very high land & some of tolerable[4] extent At 7[h] The Isl[d] that bore West now bore WbS or true West & in this lat[d] it opened

[16]

1 The last of Hayward's entries.

2 The islands shown on the sketch map are as follows; at the centre is
   Makongai, made up of two islands. To the north-east is Koro, to the south-
   east Wakaya and beyond it Mbatiki; to the south-south-west Ovalau, to the
   south-west-$\frac{1}{2}$-west Naingani and beyond it the great extent of Viti Levu.
   To the west-$\frac{1}{2}$-south is Passage Rock and north-by-west of it is the other
   large island of Vanua Levu. This sketch must be the original version of the
   second chart sent to Banks, now in the Mitchell Library, and reproduced in
   Henderson, facing p. 134. The '$\frac{1}{2}$' in the above bearings refers to half a point
   on the compass, a point being 11°15'.

3 Passage Island at the south-eastern extremity of the reef extending from
   Vanua Levu.

4 Viti Levu, the largest of the Fiji Islands.

13th : *A Jack at the Foretop Gallant mast head will be an answer to all signals made from the Shores that such signals are seen.*
14th : *Besides Anchorage, Wood and Water are the particular things to be attend'd to.*

8th March 1788[1]

& showed two Isl^{ds}: it then, the opening bore WSW nearly[2]

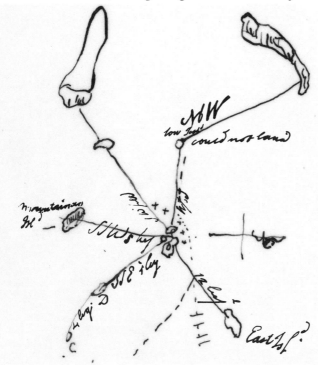

[This map has been traced from the original in order to separate it from the text it was sketched over.]

Hauled in for the Center Isles – Saw signs of Inhabitants afraid to land. Steered away for a small Isl^{d}[3] at 9^{h}: 35' At 10^{h}:3/4 Saw another large Mount^{s} Isl^{d} SWbS 10 leag^{s}[4]

[17]

1 See the note identifying the islands in the sketch map. The island 'of no value' is Passage Island. It should be noted that the Admiralty log is not as informative as the Mitchell Library's version with respect to the passage through the Fiji Islands.

At Noon Small Isl.d SEbS½E 2 Miles Center Isls East 5 leag.s A Large
Isl.d SbE½E 8 leag.s – A small one S3/4W 6 Leg.s A large Isl.d SSW1/4
W to W 10 leag.s – Another Isl.d NbW½W 9 or 10 leag.s – Dangerous
navig.n bad shoals – Attempted to land but seeing the Isl.d was of no value
bore away[1]

[The calculations which form the rest of the original material on this page will be
found with the navigational notes for 6 May.]

[18]

1 Bligh is now sufficiently organised to start keeping the notebook in the conventional log form, with some minor abbreviations. The columns, from the left, are for the hour of the day, starting at one in the afternoon, the hourly reading of the log-line in knots and fathoms, the courses steered and the wind direction. The right-hand part of the page is reserved for brief remarks.

2 This was in fact another high part of Vanua Levu, to be recognised as such an hour or so later. In this line and the following, although Bligh's entry is obviously correct, the original shows a series of diagonal strokes which would normally be interpreted as a cancellation of that part of the statement. It is difficult to explain their presence here.

3 This was near the western edge of the reef extending from Vanua Levu across which Bligh had been sailing since noon. There was, unknown to Bligh, a clear water passage about five miles south of his track.

4 The Northern Yasawas, the westernmost islands of the Fiji group.

5 Round Island, 500 feet high and about fifteen miles a little north of west from the northern tip of Yasawa Island.

6 Viti Levu.

7 Round Island again.

8 Kinsilk Rock and Timboor Islet. Bligh has now 'lost' thirty-three minutes of longitude since Tofua.

9 The two sailing canoes were thought by Bligh to be similar to those used by the Tongans. In fact the Tongans used the Fijian-built canoes which were superior to their own, see Bligh's description, in great detail, in the journal entry for 25 April 1789, made at Nomuka. The canoes involved in the chase were probably the asymmetrically hulled 'drua'; they had a house built on a platform and were not carrying many people so far as Bligh could determine, although the type was capable of holding a considerable number of crew. This canoe episode is used by Fryer, in his journal, to criticise Bligh, whom he accuses of excessive panic which he did not hide from his companions. Lebogue, the oldest member of the launch's people, according to Fryer openly chastised his captain, for which he was reprimanded by Fryer. This is one of the several occasions on which Bligh, if Fryer is accepted, was not as cool and collected as his own account would have us believe; see the landfall at the Barrier Reef, the Sunday Island argument and the Roti Island decision below.

H	K	F	Courses	Wind	Thursd.ᵞ 7ᵗʰ May 1789¹
1	3		NWbN	ENE	Mod. & fair.
2	3				
3	3		"	"	Saw another Isl.ᵈ to the NNW²
4	3		WNW	"	
5	3	3			the above Isl.ᵈ we found join to the one set at Noon NbW½W
6	1 / 2	5 / 2	WbN		At 5¾ – The extrem.ˢ of the above Island from NbW½W to NE½E
7	3	6			Served a Gill of water & a bit of bread –
8	4	4			
9	4	2			Land as far as SWbW on the S.º & NW½W on the north pas.ᵈ over a reef wᵗʰ 4 feet water³
10	4	2			
11	4				
12	4	4			
1	4				light squalls
2	3	4			
3	3	3			At day discovered land to leward from WNW to WSW like numbers of high Rocky Isl.ᵈˢ⁴ & some low land from 8 to 4 leag.ˢ dis.ᵗ – A high round Hill Isl.ᵈ⁵ NNW 6 leag.ˢ & land SSE the same as set SWbW last night⁶
4	3				
5	4				
6	3			NE	
7	3		NNW	–	
8	3		NWbN	NEbN	
9	2	¼	NW	NNE	
10	1 / 1		WNW / NNW	NE	At 9ʰ½ h. Extrem.ˢ Land to lew.ᵈ NW 5 leag.ˢ to SWbW½W a high Rock 5 leag.ˢ – High Isl.ᵈ NbE⁷
11	2	4			
12	2	4			Cloudy & Varie W.ᵗ Curr. sets us towards the Shore two small Isl.ˢ WNW 2 Miles being the north extreme of the land⁸ – Saw two sailing cannoes coming to us⁹ – Out oars to get from them Souther.ᵗ Land SbW

[19]

1 The trade wind.

[H	K	F	Courses	Wind]	Frid.y 8th. May
1	3		NW	NNE	Cloudy & Light Winds. – Kept rowing Cannoes in chace
2	3	– –		–	D.o left off chace
3	2	– –		–	Cloudy. Rain & Thunder saved 6 gall.s water. Served a bit of Pork for dinner & quenched our thirsts – Troublesome Isles EbS ½S & 3 leag.s – The Extr.s of the land SEbE ½E to SbE 7 or 8 leag.s – Cloudy W.r
4	1	" "		Calm	
5	2	" "			
6	2	" "			
7	2	"			
8	2	"			
9	5	"	WNW	NNE	Rowed offshore untill 7h.
10	5				Served a Spoonfull of Rum & a Gill of Cocoanut Milk, being all wet. –
11	4	4			
12	4	4			
1	3	6			
2	3	6			
3	3	4			
4	3	4			Squally with Rain
5	3	4			Fair began to dry our wet Cloaths every one being very uncomfortable served a bit of Bread for breakfast & a Gill Coca Nut Milk
6	3	6			
7	3				
8	3				
9	3	2			
10	3				
11	3				
12	3				Fair pleas. Trade[1] & smooth water ½ oz of Pork 1 oz Bread & a Gill of Coconutt for dinner

Lat Obs.d 16.04

[20]

[H	K	F	Courses	Wind]	Saturd.ʸ 9 May 1789
1	2	6	WbN	NNE	Fair pleas.ᵗ Trade & smooth water. –
2	2	2			
3	2	2	″		Empl.ᵈ cleaning the Boat & drying cloaths
4	2	2			
5	2			NE	
6	2	4	–	–	Served a Gill of Water & ½ oz of Bread for Supper
7	2	4			Sang a Song & went to Sleep
8	3				
9	2	6			
10	2	4			
11	2	4			
12	2	4	″	EbS	
1	2	4			
2	3				
3	2	4			
4	3	–			
5	2	2	″	″	
6	3		″	″	Served a Gill of Cocoanut Milk for Breakfast
7	2	7			
8	2	4			
9	3				
10	4				
11	3	4			
12	4				Fine W.ʳ

Lat Obs.ᵈ 15°.47′S
Long 176:35E

[21]

Sketch map of the island of Makongai, Fiji, with the boat channel mentioned by Bligh on 6 May separating its two parts. See [16], also map of the Fiji Islands [17] and note 2 corresponding.

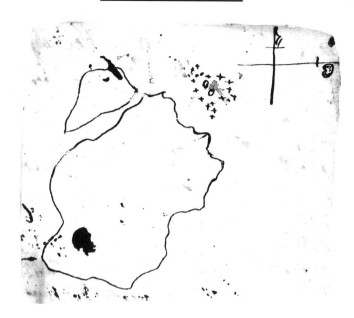

[The calculations which form the rest of the original material on this page will be found with the navigational notes for 10 May.]

[23]

1 'two' is meant here.

2 Bligh could not maintain his course of west-by-north and had to alter a point to starboard to bring the wind, which had veered to south-south-east, and the high seas more astern. A similar problem was encountered next morning just after daylight. The journal reads 'we spent a very distressing Night without Sleep ... the Sea was constantly breaking over us and we had no Choice how to steer for we were obliged to keep before the Waves to avoid filling the Boat.' There were three such nights in all, during which the launch was in great danger of foundering. It was not until 9 a.m. on the 12th that the wind and sea started to drop, to become almost calm, though it was still cold and overcast at noon.

[H	K	F	Courses	Wind]	Sundy 10 May 1789
1	2	2	WbN	EbS	Fine Wr Four coconutts for Dinner
2	2	4			
3	2	6			
4	2	2			
5	3			"	Served a Bit of Bread & a Gill of water
6	3	2			
7	3			SE	Cloudy
8	3				
9	3	4	WNW	SSE	Squally much Rain Thundr & Lightg Saved to[1] breakers of Water came of the course[2] altered – Served a teaspoonfull of Rum to each person
10	3				
11	3				
12	3			SE	
1	3	6	WbN		
2	3	6			
3	4				
4	4				
5	3	6			
6	3	6		SSE	Squally & Rain & Much Sea – Kept before it
7	3	6			A Bit of bread & a Gill of Water for breakfast
8	4	"		"	
9	4		NWbW		Very wet & uncomfortable –
10	4				
11	4				
12	4				Cloudy Wr & much Sea cant keep our course

Latd Obsd 15° 17′S

[24]

[H	K	F	Courses	Wind]	Mond.ʸ 11 May
1	4		NWbW½W	SSE	Squally & much Sea
2	4		–		Course West but obliged to keep before the Sea
3	4				
4	5	"			A bit of Pork & Bread for Dinner
5	4		WbN		Fresh Gales & Cloudy.
6	4	"		"	a bit of bread for Supper
7	5				Very Wet no dry Cloaths
8	5				
9	5				Strong Gale & much Sea
10	5				Reckon to have steer.ᵈ upon the whole no better than WbN
11	5				
12	5				Heavy Rain
1	4				Very cold & wet cons.ᵗˡʸ shipping Seas & bailing. –
2	4				
3	4				
4	3				
5	2	4	–	–	Served a teaspoonful of Rum & a bit of bread
6	2	4			
7	4				
8	5				Cloudy & Hard Gale & high Sea frequently run.ᵍ over our stern
9	5				
10	5				
11	5				
12	5				Some Sun Shine All of us Wet & uncomfortable

Lat.ᵈ Obs.ᵈ 14.50

[25]

1   Gannets are large plunge-diving marine birds with long narrow wings of the family Sulidae, related to cormorants, pelicans, tropic-birds and frigate-birds. (Peter Slater, *A Field Guide to Australian Birds, Non-Passerines*, Adelaide, 1970, p. 203.)

2   The log at this point mentions the men as 'shivering'.

3   Tropic birds and sheerwaters: the tropic-bird is a medium-sized plunge-diving bird with two long tail streamers. The red-tailed variety (*Phaeton rubricauda*) breeds on Raine Island and in North Queensland. The shearwater is a marine bird with narrow wings that glides close to the surface, which it occasionally breaks, hence the name. (Peter Slater, *op. cit.*, p. 173 and p. 212.) Bligh probably means the wedge-tailed shearwater (*Puffinus pacificus*).

[H	K	F	Courses	Wind]	Tuesd.ʸ 12 May 1789
1	4	4	West	SE	Strong Gale & high Sea. Shipping much water & everyone wet. –
2	4	4			
3	4	4			
4	4	4			½ oz pork & a bit of bread & a Gill water for dinner
5	4	"			Saw a Gannet[1] & a piece of Wood
6	4				
7	4	2			
8	4	4			Much Rain & Cold
9	4	4			
10	4	4			
11	4	4			
12	4	4			d.ᵒ
1	3	4			Cloudy
2	3	4			
3	3	4			
4	3	4			
5	3	4			Cons.ᵗ Rain & Cold
6	3	4		NNE	
7	3	4			
8	3	4			Very wet, served a bit bread & a little Rum – One man compl.ᵈ cholick
9	2	6			
10	2	4			
11	1	4			Varie.ᵈ
12	1				Calm & very Cloudy – being[2] uncomfortably Wet. – No Sun See Fish but can catch none – Tropic Birds & Sheerwaters.[3] – Dined on a bit of bread and a Gill of Water.

89

[27]

1 *Barringtonia asiatica* is the most common species, the four-angled fruit
   of which is frequently washed ashore along North Queensland beaches.
   (Information courtesy of the National Herbarium of New South Wales.) John
   Reinhold Forster, whose patron was Daines Barrington, sailed with Cook
   on his second voyage, as scientific observer and naturalist.

2 This is another name for the frigatebird, a large tropical seabird, with
   large wings and forked tail, which feeds and drinks in flight. Both the Greater
   and Lesser Frigatebird inhabit the area where Bligh made his observation.
   They are, respectively, *Fregata minor* and *Fregata ariel*. (Peter Slater,
   op. cit., pp. 210-211.)

[H	K	F	Courses	Wind]	Wedned.ʸ 13 May 1789
I		4	W	SE	Dark Cloudy W.ʳ Miserable empl.ᵈ wringing our wet Cloths but the W.ʳ so moist nothing will dry. –
2		4			
3		4	NW	SE	
4		4			
5	3	″	WbN	SWbS	Saw a fruit floating the Baringtonia of Forster.[1]
6	3	″	″	″	
7	4	2	West	S.º	
8	4	2	″	″	Dark Cloudy W.ʳ & find ourselves very cold.
9	5				
10	4	2			
11	5				
12	4	2		SSE	Squally constantly Shipping Water & most uncomfortably Wet & Cold
1	3	6			
2	3	2			
3	3	4	W½S		
4	3	4			
5	3	2			
6	3		W½N	S.º	
7	4				Cloudy W.ʳ & Squalls. Empl.ᵈ drying Cloaths. –
8	3	4			
9	3	6			Bread & Water for breakfast
10	4	″	WbN	SbW	Saw Man of War Bird[2] & fruits floating
11	4	″			
12	4				D.º W.ʳ Indiff.ᵗ Obs.ⁿ – Bread & Water for dinner at the rate of 2 oz per Man a Day & a Gill of Water. –

Obs. 14° 17′S.

[28]

1 The islands shown in Bligh's sketch map, page [30], are now known as set
   out below. The first equivalents to Bligh's designations are those of Admiralty
   chart 1575 (current) the second, bracketed, are those of *The Times Atlas:*
   'Large Island' is Vanoua Lava (Vanoua Lava), 'West Island' is Parapara
   (Ureparapara), 'East Island' is Motlav (Saddle Island), 'North Rocks' is Mota
   Island (Mota). The unnamed island at the bottom of the map is Santa Maria
   (Santa Maria). All are in the Banks Group, so named by Bligh after his patron.

2 Bligh has wrongly identified the conical hill, Mota, with the Pico de Averdi
   shown just north of the north-easterly extremity of the New Hebrides on
   Bougainville's track on Cook's 'Chart of the Southern Hemisphere showing
   the tracks of some of the most distinguished navigators...' in his *A voyage
   towards the South Pole... in... the* RESOLUTION *and* ADVENTURE *in the years
   1772, 1773, 1774 and 1775...*, London, 1777. Bligh would no doubt have
   studied this work when preparing the BOUNTY's intended home voyage from
   Tahiti through Torres Straits. Pico de Averdi on Cook's chart is actually
   Bougainville's Pic de l'Etoile, the modern Mera Lava. I am grateful for the
   particular assistance of Bruce Semler in tracing this identification.

[H	K	F	Courses	Wind]	Thursd.ʸ 14 May 1789
1		W	SbW	Fresh Breezes & Cloudy
2	4				
3	4	–	WbS	S.º	Got our Cloaths tolerably dry – What things I had Saved rotten w.ᵗʰ wet
4	4				
5	4				
6	4	"	"	"	Bread & Water for Supper
7	4				
8	4				
9	4				
10	4				
11	4				
12	4				
1	3	6	West	SbW	At 6.ʰ Saw land from SWbS 7 leag.ˢ to NWbW¾W 5 leag.ˢ – Three rem.ʳ Hills the Northernmost the smallest & most Conical WbS¾S WbS½S & W¾S 4 leag.ˢ – High Land.ˢ & Isl.ᵈˢ¹ –
2	4				
3	4	1			
4	3	6			
5	3	6			
6	3	4			
7	4	4	NWbN		
8	4	4	"	S.E	Very cloudy Mod. Breezes
9	4	4	"	"	The extr.ˢ of the land W½N to SW½S 4 leag.ˢ the s.º extreme being the Conical Hill (I. Averdi)² South land set at first not in sight
10	4	4	NWbW		
11	4	4			
12	5	"	WNW		At Noon Conical Hill & north Ex.ᵗ as set before S½E 4 leag. large Isl.ᵈ SSW½W & W land West 7 leag.ˢ A Small Isl.ᵈ NWbN 4 leag.ˢ

[29]

1 See note 1 to page [29] for the modern names of these islands.

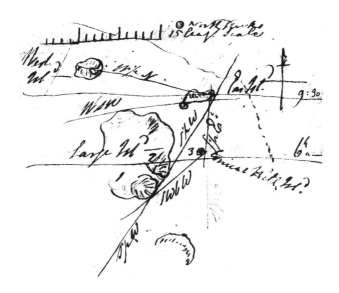

[Sketch map of the Banks Islands[1]]

On the East side of the West! Isl^d appeared a fine Harbour, formed by the whole Isl^d forming like a Crescent The Points shut on at SbW & NbE – The land is High & slopes all round to the Bottom like a Bowl. – The whole Country seems to be fertile and woody and Inhabited.

[30]

1 Probably Toga, in the Torres Islands.

2 A reference to the probably inaccuracy of the noon sextant sight of the sun. (See note on navigational calculations, 15 May.)

3 The booby belongs to the same family as the gannet, but inhabits tropical and semitropical regions. Its name is said to be derived from the Portuguese word for fool, because of its trustful behaviour near man. Three varieties, the Red-footed, Masked and Brown Booby, all *Sula*, inhabit the area traversed by Bligh. The last two range across Northern Australia into the Indian Ocean. The noddy is a dark-coloured tropical tern of the genus *Anous*, of which three species are known in Australia. The White-capped Noddy (*Anous minutus*), thirteen inches long, is the one most likely to have been seen by Bligh. It is so lacking in fear of man as to be considered either stupid or sleepy. (Peter Slater, *op. cit.* pp. 203-205, pp. 337-338.)

H	K	F	Courses	Wind	Friday 15 May 1789
1	5	"	W.ˡ	S.E	Fresh Breeze & Dark Gloomy Wʳ.
2	5	"			
3	5	"	WBN		
4	5	"	"		at 4ʰ. Conical Hill Islᵈ. SE½E Eastᵗ. Islᵈ. SEbE Largest Islᵈ. SSE Westermᵗ. Islᵈ. SbW 4 leagˢ. & North Rock seen at Noon NE½N
5	4	3	WSW		
6	4	"	"	"	
7	4	4			Saw a smoak
8	5				
9	4	2			Bread & Water for supper
10	5				SWbW our Course but the Sea will not let us keep it
11	4	2			
12	5		"	"	Squally
1	5		"	"	Saw an Islᵈ. WNW 5 leagˢ. off tolerably High¹ –
2	5				
3	5				
4	4	4			
5	6	"			
6	5	"			
7	4	6			The Islᵈ. seen at 1ʰ. – NE 10 leagˢ. –
8	4	4			
9	5		WbS		Squally with much Rain & Sea – All wet – Bread & water for breakfast. –
10	4	4			
11	4	6			Fresh Gales
12	5				Dark cloudy Wʳ. No certain [sight]² – Gannets Boobys, Noddies³ Men of War Birds. – But can see no Land. – Bread & water for Dinner

Obsᵈ. 13.55 S

[31]

1 The sail has been reduced to its smallest area by the use of the row of reef points or hanks further from its foot; see note 1, page [9] Sunday, 3 May.

2 Bligh was worried lest the need to run before the wind would take him too far north and put him on the coast of New Guinea, 'in which case most probably an End to our Voyage would soon be the consequence.' To avoid this he took every opportunity, between squalls, to steer to the southward of his intended course.

3 Mother Carey's Chickens, the name given by sailors to a petrel, *Procellaria pelagica*, supposed to be seen before storms. (*The Oxford Companion to Ships and the Sea*, p. 561.)

H	K	F	Courses	Wind	16ᵗʰ May Saturdʸ 1789
1	5	4	WSW	SE	Fresh Gales & Cloudy wᵗʰ squalls & Rain – Much Sea –
2	6				
3	6				
4	5	4			
5	5	4	WbS		Close reefed M. Sail.¹ –
6	5	"	WSW		Supped on bread & Water
7	4	6			Sea breaking over us – Very wet & Cold. –
8	4	2			
9	4		WbN		In Main Sail – Squally heavy sea cannot keep our course or see which makes our steering very bad.² –
10	3				
11	2	"			
12	4	4			
1	4	6			
2	4	2			
3	4				
4	4	–	WSW	SEbS	Moon light
5	4				
6	4	3			Set Main Sˡ being wet & Cold. – Mother Careys Chicken³ –
7	3	5			
8	3	5			Dark Cloudy. Wʳ & Squalls Rain – Bread & water for breakfast
9	3	4			
10	3	4			
11	4				
12	4				

Lat Obsᵈ 13°: 33Sᵒ   Fair & Cloudy. dryed Cloaths Saw a Booby
     165:52 E   Noddy & M. Carey Chicken –
                 Bread & Pork for Dinner Sea from SE.

[33]

1 The Admiralty *Pilot* shows a tendency for a north-westerly current to flow
   in this area although a few degrees of longitude further west the current takes
   a marked south-westerly direction. (See *Australia Pilot*, Vol. III,
   1973, pp. 16-17.)

H	K	F	Courses	Wind	Rem^s Sund^y. 17th May 1789
1	4	–	SWbW	SEbS	Fresh Breezes & Cloudy. Steered SW to counteract the Current[1]
2	4		SW		
3	4	6	"	"	Sea high – Bailing & shiping Water.
4	4	4	"		
5	4	6	"	"	
6	5	"	"	"	Bread & Water for Sup[per]
7	3	4			
8	3	4	"	"	Storms of Thunder Light^g & heavy Rain. –
9	3	4			
10	3	4			
11	3	4			Distress^d for want of light to see our Course. No Stars to be seen. –
12	3	4			
1	4	4			
2	4	4			
3	4	4			
4	4	6			
5	5				
6	5				
7	4				
8	4				D^oW^r. Served a teaspoonfull of Rum & a morsel of Bread. –
9	4				Wet & Cold.
10	3	4			Water Spout almost on board of us. –
11	3	4			
12	4	"			D^oW^r. Sky dreadfully black all round us – Bread & a ½ oz of Pork for Dinner. –
	100				

| | | | No Obsⁿ. | Wet & Cold. |

[34]

1 The log and journal read 'Dark dismal Night No Stars – Steering as the Sea directs us' and 'nothing but the Wind and Sea to direct our Steerage'.

H	K	F	Courses	Wind	Mond.ʸ 18 May 1789
1	1		SW	East	Light winds. Gloomy W.ʳ & heavy Rain. – Very wet & Cold Boobies & a kind of Gulls abᵗ
2	2				
3	3	7		SEbE	
4	4				
5	4	4			
6	4		″		Fresh Gales dark W.ᵗ & squally great Sea from SE breaking over us – Very wet & Cold. Bread & Water for Sup.ʳ
7	5				
8	5				
9	5		″		Steering by the Sea not able to see the compss.¹ –
10	6				
11	5	4	″	SE	Heavy Rain – Nothing to Shelter us – very wet & Cold & pain in our Bones.
12	5				
1	5				
2	5				
3	5				
4	4	6			
5	4	6			
6	5				
7	4	6		E.ˡ	
8	4	4	″	SE.	Ceased Raining – Dark Cloudy W.ᵗ much Sea. began to wring our wet Cloaths. –
9	5	″ ″	″		
10	4	6			
11	3	4		E.ˡ	
12	3	4		ENE	
	106				Squally wᵗʰ. Rain Bread & water for Dinner – Some Birds, Boobies & Noddies No Obs.

[35]

H	K	F	Courses	Winds	Tuesday 19th. May 1789
1	3	6	WbS	ENE	Squally with Rain wch. keeps us uncomfortably wet
2	4				
3	5		" "		Confused Sea
4	4	4			
5	4	4	West		
6	4	4		NE	Dark cloudy Wr. Bread & Water for Supper. –
7	4	4			
8	4	4			
9	4				
10	4		"	"	
11	4		"	"	Squally & Rain
12	2		"	ENE	
1	3		"	"	Constant heavy Rain & Lightning. –
2	3				
3	3				
4	3		"	"	Miserably Cold
5	3	4			
6	4	4			
7	4	4	"	"	Fresh Breezes & Cloudy began to wring our wet Cloaths.
8	4	4	"	"	Bread & Water for Breakft. Bone Complaints.
9	4		" "	"	
10	4		" "	"	
11	4		" "	"	Squally
12	4		" "	ESE to ENE	Constant Rain. Bd. & ½ oz Pork for Dinner – No Obs.

[37]

[H	K	F	Courses	Winds]	Wed.y 20 May
1	3	4	West	ENE	Mod. & Rainy W.r which distresses us exceed.ly
2	3	4			
3	3				
4	2	4			Deluge of Rain
5	3	"			
6	3	"	"	"	D.o W.r We now dread the Night being so cold & wet. Served Bread
7	2	6			
8	4	5			
9	3	2	"	"	Frequent Squalls of heavy Rain. –
10	3	2			
11	3	2			
12	3	2			
1	3	2			
2	4				
3	3	4			
4	5		"	"	
5	4		"	"	D.o W.r Cold & Wet served a teaspoonful of Rum
6	4				
7	4				
8	4		"	"	Bread & Water for Break.
9	3	4			Boobies Man of War Birds & Kind of Gulls.
10	2	4			
11	2	4			
12	3		"	"	"	

82

Lat Obs.d 14°49S

Fair W.r Empl.d drying our wet cloaths.
Served Bread & water for dinner

[39]

1 'sharks' in log.

2 These figures, upside down in pencil in the original, probably show
Bligh's estimate of his noon position on 4 May. His actual DR position for that
time was 18°55'S, 177°44'W.

[H	K	F	Courses	Wind]	Thursd.ʸ 2 1 May
1	3		W¹⁄₂N	East	Fresh Breezes & Cloudy W.ʳ –
2	3	4			
3	3	6	"	"	Constant Rain – Many Birds & Fish – Boobies Noddies – Tropic Gulls – almost able to catch them w.ᵗʰ our Hand Many Shirk¹ Dolphins & other fish but cannot catch any. –
4	4	4			
5	4	4			
6	4	"			
7	4	"			
8	4				
9	4				Supper as usual
10	4		WbN	"	Storm of Rain
11	4				
12	4		" "	"	Dismal dark Rainy W.ʳ not able to see the compss steer.ᵍ by the sea & suppose on our Course Miserably Wet & the Rain so heavy scarce able to keep the Boat free by bailing. –
1	3	6			
2	3	6	W¹⁄₂N		
3	3	4			
4	4			SE.ˡ	Lat. 19.39
5	4		"		16
6	4				37
7	5			ESE	177.27W²
8	5		"	"	Breakfast as usual – Very Wet & Cold. –
9	5				
10	5		" "	"	W.ʳ clearing
1 1	5				
12	5				Fresh Gales & Cloudy W.ʳ w.ᵗʰ some Sunshine. – Empl.ᵈ drying Cloaths

100

Lat Obs.ᵈ 14.29S

[40]

1 Fryer says that Bligh sat under a tree on Restoration Island almost all the last day there correcting the Prayer Book, being supplied with food and water at intervals by Midshipman Hallett. After leaving the island Bligh said a new prayer each night and morning. Fryer appears to be referring to an actual Prayer Book in Bligh's possession.

Prayer[1]

O Lord our heavenly Father almighty and everlasting God,* who has safely brought us to the beginning of this day; In and through the merits of our blessed Saviour through whom we are taught to ask all things, – We thy unworthy Servants prostrate ourselves before thee & humbly ask thee forgiveness of our sins and transgressions.

We most devoutly thank thee for our preservation & are truly conscious that only through thy Divine Mercy we have been saved – We supplicate thy glorious majesty to accept our unfeigned Prayers & thanksgivings for thy gracious Protection. – Thou hast shewed us wonders in the deep, that we might see how powerfull & gracious a God thou art, how able & ready to help those who trust in thee. Thou hast given us strength & fed us & hast shewn how both Winds & Seas obey thy command, that we may learn

[41]

even from them to hereafter obey thy holy word and to do as thou hast ordered.

We bless and glorify thy name for this thy mercy in saving us from perishing, and we humbly beseech thee to make us as truly sensible of such thy Almighty goodness that we may be always ready to express a thankfullness not only by our Words, but also by our lives in living more obedient to thy Holy Commandments.

Continue O Lord we beseech thee, through the mediation of our blessed Saviour Jesus Christ, this thy goodness towards us, – strengthen my mind & guide our Steps – Grant unto us health and strength to continue our Voyage, & so bless our miserable morsel of Bread, that it may be sufficient for our undertaking.

O Almighty God relieve us from our extreme distress, such as men

[42]

never felt, – conduct us through thy mercy to a Safe Haven, and in the End restore us to our disconsolate Families and Friends. We promise O Lord with full and contrite hearts never to forget thy great mercies vouchsafed unto us – We promise to renew our unfeigned thanks at thy Divine Altar & amend our lives according to thy holy word. – And now Almighty God as thou hast given us grace at this time to make our common supplications unto thee & hast promised that to those who ask in thy Son our Saviours name thou wilt grant their request; fulfill O Lord we beseech thee the desires & Petions of thy Servants as may be most expedient for them granting us in this world a knowledge of thy truth & in the World to come life everlasting through the Merits of our Blessed Mediator and Redeemer Jesus Christ. Amen – Our Father. –
*Receive us this Night into thy almighty protection

[43]

1 Bligh's remarks in the journal, which in this period certainly conceals little, reveals a man not so self-confident as we usually see. 'If ever', he writes, 'Men experienced the power of goodness of Divine providence we do at this instant in a most emminent degree, and I presume to say our present situation would make the boldest Seaman tremble that ever lived... as the least error in the Helm would in a moment be our destruction –'

H	K	F	Courses	Wind	Frid.ʸ 22 May 1789
1	5	2	W½S	ESE	Fresh Gales & Fine Wʳ. wᵗʰ. a high Sea from the SE
2	5	2			
3	5		WbS		Greatly refreshed by the fine Wʳ. – Empl. drying our Wet Cloaths. –
4	4	4			
5	4	6			
6	4	6		"	Cloudy Wʳ. – Served our proportion of bread & water for Supper
7	5	4			
8	5	4	"	"	Ship.ᵈ many Seas – All Wet & cold.ˡ –
9	5	4			
10	5	4			
11	5	4			
12	5	4			
1	5	4			
2	5	4			
3	5	4			
4	5	4	"		
5	5	4		SE.ˡ	
6	5	4		"	Very Squally & much sea always bailing.
7	5	4			
8	5	4	"	"	Bread & Water for Breakfast
9	5	4	W½S	SbE	Squally & Rain – Cant keep our Course
10	5	4		SE	
11	5	4	WbN	SSE	A Heavy Sea cant keep our Course
12	5	4		ESE	Fair Wʳ. Sea breakᵍ over us. Under Single
	131		Fresh Gales		Reef Fore Sail

[45]

1 'The misery of this day', reads the journal, 'has exceeded the preceding –
   The Night was dreadfull The Sea flew over us with great force and kept us
   bailing with horror and anxiety'. Bligh made much of his discovery that the
   rain-soaked clothes were warmer if wrung out in salt water, the sea being in
   the vicinity of 27 degrees Celsius or 80 Fahrenheit.

H	K	F	Courses	Wind	Saturdy. 23d. May 1789
1	5		WbN	SSE	Fresh gales & fair Wr. but a high breaking Sea which keeps us constantly Wet & bailing and not able to keep our course. –
2	5				
3	5			So.	
4	5				
5	5		West		
6	5		"	"	
7	5		"	"	Squally with Rain
8	5		"	"	
9	6		WbN	SE	
10	6				
11	5		WNW	ESE	
12	5				Sea breaking all over us – constantly Bailing
1	5	"	WbN	SSE	
2	5				
3	5	4			
4	5		West	SE	
5	4	"			
6	3	4	"	"	Squally Wr. Have past a dreadf.l bad night. All numb.d with the Cold & Wet – Not a dry Thread – Began to wring Wet Cloaths¹
7	5	"			
8	5		W½N	"	
9	5			SSE	Served Rum & Bread
10	5			S.l	
11	4	5	WbN	SE	
12	5	"			Fresh Gales & fair Wr. but Sea so high every instant in danger of filling – Bread as usual for

Latd. Obsd. 13°.44S   dinner – One Man Complaing.

[46]

1 Both sails were reduced to their smallest area.

2 This was the first time for fifteen days that the men had enjoyed any warmth from the sun.

H	K	F	Courses	Wind	Rem.s Sund.y 24 May 1789
1	5	4	WNW	SSE	Fresh Gale & much Sea from the South
2	5	2			
3	5	2			Mother Careys Chicken
4	5				
5	4	6	WbS	S°.	Under Close Reef M.S. & F.S¹
6	4	6			Cloudy Cold Even.g Not so much Sea & steer across it very well
7	5				
8	4	4			Saw two Noddies & a Booby
9	5				Bread & Water for Supper
10	4	6		SSE	
11	5				
12	5		"		Fine Night but very cold
1	5				
2	5				
3	5				
4	5				
5	5				
6	5				
7	4	4			
8	4	"			Fine W.r – Men of War & Tropic Birds – Some Fish – Bread etc for Breakfast –
9	4	2			
10	4	2			
11	4	4			
12	5	"			Fine W.r Empl.d drying Cloaths for the 1st time found any warmth from the Sun² Bread & oz Pork for Din.r
			Lat.d 13°.33'S		

[47]

1 An abbreviation of Mother Carey.

2 Bligh was worried about the possibility of missing Timor and having to carry on to Java; he therefore extended the twenty-nine days of bread left at the existing ration of one-eighth of a pound daily to forty-three days at one-twelfth.

3 The noddy, 'the size of a small pigeon', was divided with its entrails into eighteen portions which were then chosen at random by the men, so that pure chance determined the quality of the particular fragment obtained. This was the first of several birds caught by hand, most of them being the larger booby.

H	K	F	Courses	Wind	Rem.ˢ Mond.ʸ 25 May 1789
1	4	6	WbS	SSE	Fine Wʳ. & a Cool Air – Some Boobies – Men of War Birds – MKᵗChicken. –
2	4				
3	4				
4	4				Overhauled our Bread & found 43 days Bread at the rate of weight of 2 Musket Balls, or 1/12 of a lb to each Man per Day.
5	4	4			
6	4	4			
7	4	4	"		Saw a Gannet. –
8	4	4	"		Our Issues now will be 1/12 of lb Bread & a small Wine Glass of Water at Breakfast & Dinner & only Water at Supper²
9	4	2			
10	4	4			
11	5				
12	5				
1	4				Every one complains of Costiveness most of us 18 Days without an evacuation
2	4				
3	4	4			
4	4	4			
5	4				Caught a Noddy by Hand³
6	4				
7	5				
8	4	4			Flying showers of Rain
9	5				Bread for Breakfast
10	5				
11	5				
12	5				Squally Noddies & Tropic Gulls

Lat.ᵈ 13°.32S

[49]

1 It was just as likely to have come from the north. Captain Ware observed large trees near the reef in a southerly current. (R. W. Ware, 'Child of Bounty', *Australian Boating,* no. 118, December, 1983, p. 14 of Special Supplement.)

2 Foresail and mainsail.

H	K	F	Courses	Wind	Rem.ˢ Tuesd.ʸ 26 May 1789
1	5		WbS	SSE	Fair W.ʳ & Squalls of Rain
2	5				Served the Noddy for Dinner
3	5				
4	4				
5	5				Caught a Booby by Hand
6	5				
7	5				
8	5				
9	5	60			One of the pieces of wood seen was the body
		48			of a large Tree. I imagine this to have drifted
		108			from the South.¹
10	5	3			
11	5	111			
12	5				D.ºW.ʳ
1	4				
2	4	4			Booby's the size of a good Duck & Nodies
					near that of a Pidgeon
3	5				
4	4	4			
5	4				
6	4				
7	4			SE	
8	4				Very fine W.ʳ Caught a Booby by hand. –
9	4				
10	4	4			Revived by this fair W.ʳ but very weak. –
11	4	4			Tropic Gulls, Boobies, Noddies & many
					pieces of Trees pass covered w.ᵗʰ Barnacles
12	4	4			
			Lat.ᵈ 13.41		D.ºW.ʳ under FS.ˡ & M.S.ˡ²
			Sea from S.E.		Served the Birds Raw for Dinner –

[51]

1 'squids' in the log.

H	K	F	Courses	Wind	Rem.ˢ Wednesd.ʸ 27 May [1789]
1	4		West	SE	Fine W.ʳ
2	4				
3	4				Many Noddies, Boobies & Tropic Gulls
4	4				
5	4	4			
6	4	6		ESE	Caught a Booby by hand, found several Flying Fish & Squibs¹ in his maw
7	4	4			
8	4	5			
9	4	4			
10	4	4			
11	4	4			
12	4				
1	4	4			
2	4				
3	3	6			
4	4				
5	3	6			
6	5	" "	"	"	Fine W.ʳ Many Boobies Noddies & Flying Fish –
7	5	4			
8	5	4	.		Caught a Booby – Providence seems to supply us w.ᵗʰ food we are now in great want and distress – Killed the Bird for Dinner & w.ᵗʰ the other gave us great refreshment – Gutts and every offal eat raw with great Voraciousness – These Birds are of a light brown colour & flying close in upon us, was caught by hand
9	5				
10	5				
11	5				
12	5				
	109				
	Lat Ob.ᵈ 13:°26′S				Sun powerfull People faint
	Sea from ESE				Began upon 2.ᵈ Breaker of Water

[52]

1 The reef encountered at 0100 was probably the south-eastern extremity of Tijou Reef in latitude 13°16'. At 0600 Bligh was probably fifteen miles east of the Barrier in latitude approximately 12°58'S.

2 This was Cape Direction, thought later by Bligh to be an island.

3 Given in the log as 2 to 3 cables, or 400 to 600 yards.

4 The Heming Range, which rises to 1034 feet, eight and a half miles south-west of Cape Direction.

5 Cape Weymouth, about eighteen miles distant.

H	K	F	Courses	Wind	Rem.ˢ Thursd.ʸ 28 May
1	5		West	ESE	Fine Wʳ. following Sea
2	5				
3	4	6			
4	4	4			
5	4	6			Horizon cloudy in the SW & WSW wᶜʰ. I hope indicates being near New Holland. –
6	4	6	"	"	
7	4		W½N		Served Water 2 Gills for Supper being very thirsty. –
8	4				
9	4				Saw a Gannet. –
10	4	4	"	East	
11	4	4			
12	4	4			
1	4	4	"	"	Fell in wᵗʰ a dreadfull breaking Reef WSW to WNW. Hauled the Wind & cleared it disᵗ. cable length discovered it first by the Noise of the breakers.[1]
2	4		"	NNE	
3	4		"		
4	4		"		
5	4		"		
6	4		"	"	"	At 6 Steered again for the Coast. – Nothing insight.
7	3	4	W½N	"	
8	4		"	"	"	
9	3		"	"	"	Made the Reef from NNW to SbW & Saw a Hill Disᵗ. back WbN[2] – Hauled Wind – Saw an opening 9½ʰ steered in W½N & Land only seen as before W½N 8 legˢ ½ Mile across[3] –
10	2		"	NNE	"	
	1	4	}W½N	"	
11	5		" WNW	"	Saw Land High SWbW[4]
12	4		NW	E	At 11 Bore away – Chanˡ. ESE 5 Miles. Land SWbW to NWbW Land first Seen WbS
			Latᵈ. Obsᵈ. 12°.46′		At Noon fine Wʳ. Land first seen WSW 5 or 6 leagˢ & Land farther North NWbW½W[5]

1 This entry is a reversion to the conventional practice of elaborating the
   remarks made on the log page into a longer and more informative journal
   form. This convention had been maintained, of course, in the 'fair Journal'
   that Bligh was also keeping in the launch. These comments therefore deal
   with events of Thursday 28 May.

2 The word 'with' here, and two words later, is reproduced as it occurs in
   the manuscript. Bligh probably intended to write 'we cleared without risk or
   trouble'. Fryer gives a slightly more sobering account of the episode which
   contains another criticism of Bligh's behaviour. Fryer claims he was the watch
   officer who first heard the breakers about one in the morning. Standing in the
   bows of the launch, supported by the mast, he soon saw the breakers ahead,
   whereupon he informed Bligh and at the same time got the vessel onto a
   north-north-easterly course, dipped the mainsail and put the men to the oars.
   Bligh says in his journal that he saw the breakers a quarter of a mile under his
   lee and immediately hauled the wind to the north-north-east, which rather
   deprives Fryer of the credit for the prompt action described above. According
   to the Master's account Bligh's contribution was to call out, at the height of the
   activity, 'Pull my lads we shall be Swamped.' 'Very pritty [sic] encourage-
   ments', notes Fryer, 'for people in Distress. I then called out "My lads
   Pull there is no danger." '

3 He is probably referring to Cape Direction and Cape Weymouth.

I now[1] expected to fall in with New Holl reefs every hour being determined to look for a passage & take the first opening. At 1 am fell in with
a reef w.[h] broke dreadfully but we were so providentially situated that
with[2] cleared with risk or trouble – I stood however all night to the NNE
& at daylight steered in to determine whether the reef was detached or a
part of the main reef
At 9.[h] made for the main reef & disc. an opening ½ mile wide. Stood for
it wth a strong current setting West – When in the Passage Land like an
Isl.[d] was only seen & bore W½N – The Reef to the north.[d] inclined to the
NE & to the South SSW & blue water to the North as far as I could see
– Deep water in the Channel – More land Seen & mountainous. I
endeavor.[d] to come to a Grapnel on the Reef but could not the current run
so Strong to the south. I therefore bore away as I could not keep my
ground to observe. – All happy at this Providential entry. – Expected to
take the reef – No dry ground inside reef.
The land first seen to the north insight both still look like Isl[ds][3] but
perhaps joined by lowland – too hazy to see the land to the South –
Smooth water

[55]

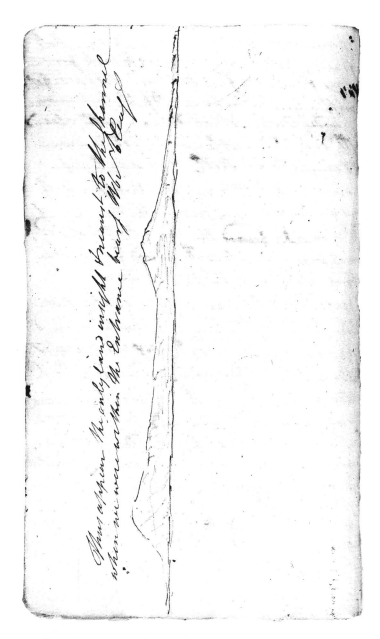

[Cape Direction and the land immediately to the south.]

Thus appears the only land insight & nearest to the Channel when we were within the Entrance bearg. WbS 6 leag[s]

[56]

1 Burke Reef.

2 Restoration Rock, three-quarters of a mile east of Restoration Island.

3 This was the north-west side of Restoration Island, so named by Bligh, 'this being the Day of Restoration of King Charles the Second and the name being not inapplicable to my present situation...'

4 Although Bligh's bearing is ten degrees in error this must be Fair Cape, which is sixteen miles from Restoration Island on a true bearing of 320 degrees.

5 Bligh is referring to the shore of Cape Weymouth, still thought by him to be an island. A later log entry refers to it as the mainland.

6 Probably Cape Griffith, 'a bold and rocky headland' in the *Pilot's* words, p. 195.

7 The small island is probably one of the Forbes Islands.

8 In this area the ebb tide runs to the south but in the south-east trade wind season the general northward pressure of current and wind results in an overall northward movement, greatest with the flood tide and least with the ebb.

9 This was a small magnifying glass carried by Bligh to read the calibrations on his sextant.

H	K	F	Courses	Wind	Remarks Friday 29 [May]
1	4		NW	E.	Fine W. –
2	4	4	NWbW		At ¾ past 3 came too at an End of a Reef¹ to try for fish
3	4	6	WNW	ESE	
4	2	6			Land first seen an Isl. S¾E 5 leag. – another with a round Top off it WbN½N –
5	4		WbN		
6					
7					At 4 find no fish bore away for Round Top Isl.²
8					At 5 Round Top Isl. No.most land NW½W & Isl. first seen SE¾S
9					
10					At ¼ past 5 Got into a Bay on the NW side of an Isl. next to Round Top & landed on a Sandy Point call Restoration point.³
11					
12					
1					
2					The Northernmost Land in sight NWbN¼N
3					8 leag.⁴ An Isl with three sandy points which
3					lies between us & the Main from NW¼N to
4					SWbS dis. a quarter of a Mile.⁵ A small Isl.
5					ab. 4 miles off was on with the northernmost
6					extremity Restoration Isl. or Isl. I am on
7					NEbN¼E¼ of Mile to SbE½ Mile. – A
8					high peeked Hill wch. I take to be part of the
9					Main SbW½W.⁶ Land to the South SbE But
10					Land first seen or Isl. of Direction lays more
11					to the East. – Found oysters & Perrywinkles
12					Supped on them a small Isl. NbW 4 or 5 leag.⁷

AM Gathered more & with one allowance of
Pork & Bread made a fine Dinner. – Hands
getting Boat in order. – Found water – Ebb
from the South.d⁸ People could hardly walk
weak – Noon much refreshed – Skelleton of a
Snake 8 feet long hung on a Tree – Great
trouble in getting a fire my read. Glass did it⁹

[58]

1 Presumably the bark gunyah.

2 Adventure Bay, in Tasmania, where Bligh had been the previous year on his
   way to Tahiti.

3 One of the widespread cabbage palms, possibly *Livistona australis*. The
   stew, a mixture of bread, a little pork, oysters and the palm cabbages, was made
   in a copper pot that one of the men had, 'with presence of mind', brought
   from the BOUNTY. Bligh was also indebted to another man who had thrown
   into the boat 'a piece of Brimestone and a Tinder Box', which later allowed
   fire to be made at will. It is not explained why it was necessary to use the
   glass on this occasion. See [58] and note 9.

4 The botanical information given here has been provided by the National
   Herbarium of New South Wales, to the Director of which, Dr L. A. S. Johnson,
   and to Mr Tony Rodd, Botanist, I make grateful acknowledgement. The
   palm tree with the edible top is probably a species of *Livistona*, or cabbage
   palm. The fern roots were either *Blechnum orientale* or *Acrostichum aureum*,
   both of which occur in swampy regions. The 'Seaside Grape' of the West
   Indies is *Coccoloba uvifera*; Bligh was probably referring to *Smilax australis*,
   which has wide, thick leaves similar to *Coccoloba*, and clusters of bluish-black
   fruits. The plant with berries like 'Bullums' was possibly a species of
   Terminalia. The tender vine with red berries was probably a plant belonging to
   the family Cucurbitaceae; 'toa' is a common name for the southern genus
   Phyllocladus, but Bligh was probably referring to *Araucaria cunninghamii*, Hoop
   Pine. 'Machineel' (Bligh uses this form in the log) refers to a plant with a milky
   sap. The most likely plant of this type on the island is *Ochrosia elliptica* in the
   family Apocynaceae. The 'wire grass' mentioned on Sunday Island and
   elsewhere could refer to a grass belonging to the genus *Eriachne*. The bean,
   also called pea, found on Sunday Island was probably *Canavalia maritima*, the
   seeds and pods of which can be eaten after thorough cooking but are poisonous
   in the raw state. Bligh guessed correctly the cause of the illness of his men.
   The 'Purow' has not been identified.
      The question whether coconuts are indigenous to Australia has been
   controversial. The most recent research, however, suggests that wild-type
   self-sown coconuts were already on the Queensland coast at the time of
   European discovery, before cultivated types were introduced. Bligh's observation supports this conclusion. See W. S. Gruezo and M. C. Harries, 'Self-
   sown Wild-type Coconuts from Australia', *Biotropica*, 16 (2),
   1984, pp. 148-151.

Variety of High & lowland Hills Woody

Round Top Isl.ᵈ a heep of Stones – left it – Got to Restoration Point ½ Mile from it. –

Only Oysters & Perrywinkles. –

No Inhabitants but signs of having been here. – Saw two wigwams weather side only covered.[1]

Saw a Pointed Stick as at Adven Bay[2] Weapons

Dug for water among some Wire Grass ab.ᵗ 200Yd.ˢ SE of Restoration point in a hollow found very good. –

Found a run sufficient to water the Ship ab.ᵗ ½ Mile more to the east.ᵈ coming from the Hills

Cut down Palm Tree Tops & found the part next the Tree good eating & did well to mix with our dinner & Stew.[3] –

Tryed Fern Roots but found them indifferent.

Saw fresh marks of Kangaroo & believe many are here.

Saw a few old pieces of Cocoa Nutts so they must be on the Main. – Kind of Seaside Grape – Berrys something like Bullums – Red Berries on a tender Vine – all eat

Toa Tree – Mangeneel-Species of the Purow[4]

Stoney Surface & sandy Soil. –

Parrots – Pidgeons – Doves & other Birds. –

[59]

1 A total of nearly 60 gallons.

2 Bligh complains in the journal that some of the men wanted to stay longer on the island, while others were anxious to continue the voyage: 'these unthankful people were no sooner saved from perishing with want and fatigue that they had forgot the mercies they had received.'

3 This latitude was the result of a good observation, according to Bligh. It is only two minutes in error, the actual figure being 12°37'S. On this occasion the sextant had an error of two, not four, minutes of arc. Bligh's longitude for Restoration Island (see calculations for 29 May) is 144° 44'E, whereas the actual figure is 143° 26'30", a difference of 1° 17'30". Taking into account the original 25 minute error for Tofua, Bligh has lost 52 1/2 minutes of longitude since that departure; since 33 of these had been lost by the time he left Fiji, the error since then is only 19 1/2 minutes, or about eighteen miles, a remarkable achievement.

Rem.ˢ in Restoration Island

Saturd.ʸ 30ᵗʰ May 1789. –
– Very fine W.ʳ Wind ESE & SE

After eating our dinner we employed the latter part of the afternoon
gathering Oysters & got sufficient with some Palm Tops to make a good
Stew for Supper & issued full 1 ½ pint of it to each Man and every one
found himself vastly better – The general complaints were a great weak-
ness & some few of a dizzyness in the head, for my own part I suffered
only a little of the former and a pain in the Pit of my Stomach. –
As the Isl.ᵈ we are on does not extend above a Mile or 1 ½ round nothing
new occured. – Part of us Slept on Shore & myself & others in the Boat –
In the Morng having only 2 lbs of Pork left I directed the oystering party
to go on for our last good dinner & with bread by Noon I offered to every
one as much as before. – They now began to com –

[60]

New Holland

plain of gathering their food I therefore prepared for Sailing – Filled the
Bar.ˡ & Four Breakers of Water,¹ and cut some necessary Spars –
Ordered some Fern Tops to be got w.ᶜʰ appeared to be cooling & may be
of service to eat raw as it will lay thirst. –
The little pork I had when we sailed we have found frequently to be
stolen & found it so now, but cannot discover the Wretch that did it. –
Kind providence protects us wonderfully but it is a most unhappy situa-
tion to be in a Boat among such discontented People who dont know
what to be at or what is best for them.²
High Water at Noon ab.ᵗ 3 feet rise

55:23	Sun alt LL
− 4	Error
55:19	
13	
55:32	
34.28	
21:49	
12.39	Lat.ᵈ of Restoration Point.³

[61]

Saturd 30th May contin.^d –

I now have 38 days allowance Bread at 1/12 lb p.^r days.

Saw many Pieces of Pumice Stone on the Shore & a very long & large
Tree hove up at the back of the Beach from whence I conclude Gales are
strong when they blow from the NW

our little well still supplies plenty of Water. –

Empl.^d a Hand mend^g the Main Sail

Saw a Bee & some Lizards. –

What Beaches we see are of a white Sand. –

The Kangooro's I believe swim from the Main from Isl.^d to Isl.^d

All the country we can see appeared rather scorched – But a pleasing
variety of high & low land & the interior part of the Main Mountainous

This Isl.^d may be known by a heap of large Rocks which form round Top
Isl.^d that lies ¼ Mile to the ESE of it.

I find the Lat. of Restoration Point to be 12°:39′S 144°:44′E –

[62]

Many Isl^{ds}. & curious projecting Rocky points along the Coast

[The calculations which form the rest of the original material on this page will be
found with the navigational notes for 1 and 2 June.]

[63]

1 The key is Quoin Island.

2 During the sixteen-hour passage from Restoration Island to Sunday Island the north-setting effect of current and tide averaged just over one knot, so that the launch was seventeen miles ahead of her reckoning when she reached Sunday Island. Because the strength of this current and tide combination was not uniform throughout the period it is difficult to plot Bligh's exact position during the hours of darkness. At 8 p.m. Fair Cape was abeam and the launch was possibly half-way between it and the long Gallon Reef. At 11 p.m. when Bligh realises the coast is sweeping back to the north-east and embaying him he must have been perilously close to Pickard Reef. From here he gradually alters course to starboard, following the trend of the shore until somewhere between 2 a.m. and 3 a.m., being close to the shore in the bay formed by the easterly extension of Cape Grenville, he tacks to the south. At 6 a.m. he is able to see his position four miles south of the Cape, from which he is able to run to the north-east and through the strait between Cape Grenville and the Home Islands, to reach Sunday Island three miles north-west of the Cape at 8 a.m.

H	K	F	Courses	Wind	Rem.ᵘ 31ˢᵗ. May 1789 [Sund.ʸ]

H K F Courses Wind   Rem.ˢ 31ˢᵗ. May 1789 [Sund.ʸ]

1 Very fine W.ʳ ESE Wind

2

3 " " "   "   Prayers

4 " " "   ESE   Sailed. Saw Natives

5 3 2 NbW   Strong Tide in our Favor. –

6 3 2 "   "   North.ⁿ land as seen from Rest.ⁿ Isl.ᵈ & is the
same now & makes a fair Cape WNW ¼ N
5 leag.ˢ a Key NEbN 6 Miles ¹ – Isl.ᵈ seen on
shore NbW 6 Miles Round Top Isl.ᵈ SSE ½ E
Rest.ⁿ Island SSE ¼ E 7ml.ˢ Land first seen or
I Direct S26°E just discernible.

7 4 " NW   SE+

8 3 4 NWbW

9 3 4 –WNW

10 3 4

11 3 4 NNW

12 2 6

1 2 4 N

2 2 4

3 3 4 NE   ESE   [?] At 2 Hauled the Wind find.ᵍ we were
embayed ²

4 3 4 S.ᵒ   "

5 2 4 "   "

6 2 6   North Land as seen from Res.ⁿ Isl.ᵈ SSE 7
leag.ˢ East pt. of the Main N.ᵒ 4 Miles – Islands
from N ¼ E 4 Miles to ESE 6 m.ˢ – Steered
between them & the Main – Main low &
Sandy

7 2   NEbE SEbE

8 2   N.ᵒ   –

9

10   At 8.ʰ at Sunday Isl.ᵈ North W of the Main
WbN 3 leag.ˢ S.ᵒ point S ½ E 4 Miles the Pt. I
came from

11

12

Lat Obs.ᵈ 11°58'S

[64]

1 These remarks refer to the events of Sunday 31 May as set out on the previous tabulated page.

1 Probably a spear-thrower.

2 The bearing in brackets is not in the manuscript but comes from the log. It refers to Sunday Island.

3 This is Round Point, the eastern extremity of Shelburne Bay. The next land beyond the point is over twenty miles away and was probably not visible to Bligh.

4 There are three islets in this area, the largest, Rodney Islet, being three quarters of a mile east-north-east of Round Point.

Rem^s.¹

Having eat our Dinners & every thing ready for our departure I read
prayers & returned thanks for our safety. – Just as I had done about 20
Natives came down on the opposite which I find is the Main. They were
Black and armed with Spears, I therefore left the place lest some
Cannoes & others might come & surprise us being unarmed. – They
waved & made signs & hollowing & I steered for the Isl^d seen NbW &
from thence at dusk ab^t 8 O'Clock I was abreast of Fair Cape.

Before Sun down no land could be seen without it. I therefore concluded
the coast inclined to the NW & WNW & Steered accordingly, but I
found I was mistaken & was obliged to keep hauling to the North as I
met with low land & found I was embaying myself.

At day light I found the appearance of the country all changed being all
low, some nothing but white Sand Hills & the rest not a very fertile
appearance however there were in many places Trees & small Wood.
Several Isl^{ds} now lay to the North & East and I took a channel between
the nearest & the main ab^t 1 Mile across leaving the Isl^{ds} on the Starb^d
Side – Some of these were very pretty spots & well situated for fish many
of which we sailed through but could catch none. – Seven natives

[65]

now made their appearance on the Main armed with a Spear & another
weapon.[1] They made signs to come on shore but as my situation was not
elligible I did not choose – They waved branches of some Tree or Bush
as sign of Friendship but there were some of their other motions less
friendly. – A larger Party we saw coming from a dis^t back I therefore
steered on for an Isl^d further off bearg [N½W 4 miles].[2]

At 8 O'Clock we landed to get what the Isl^d produced – From whence
the Main bore WbN 3 leag^s[3] to S½E 4 Miles full of Milk white sand
Hills – No mountainous land to be seen at the back. –

The Natives were jet Black & seemed to have rather bushy hair or wool.
I do not think their talk or voice was like Van Diemens land inhabitants.
Two Isl^{ds} off the North part of the Main in sight.[4] –

The Isl^{ds} in general are from ½ Mile round to ab^t 2 Miles. –
Found water in Hollow & an old

[66]

1 This was almost certainly a Torres Strait Islands canoe. The journal says it was built in three pieces, a separate bottom and two attached side pieces. On his second breadfruit voyage Bligh saw several Torres Strait Islanders' canoes which he observed carefully. These canoes were from 50 to 58 feet long, with a beam of 3 feet and a full depth of 2 feet. They were built in 'one piece except a kind of Gunwale to form a strait sheer – Had a stage across the Gunwale and an outrigger on each side – The Stern was a little Carved and ornamented in the head with Shells –' (Log of the PROVIDENCE, 7 September 1792). These canoes had fifteen or so men in them according to Bligh but may have been capable of holding more. The Torres Strait Islanders of Melanesian origin were great seafarers, unlike the Aborigines, although the latter had learnt how to make dugout canoes, from the Macassar men who visited north Australia, as well as outrigger craft, under the influence of the Torres Strait Islanders, but it is doubtful if they were responsible for the large craft seen by Bligh.

2 William Dampier, in the ROEBUCK, was on the western and northern coast of Australia in 1699 and formed a very unfavourable impression of it and its inhabitants. Unlike Bligh, Cook said (entry for 23 August 1770) that the Queensland coast north of 25°S was much better than Dampier's description of the other side of the continent.

3 Sunday Island is 157 feet high.

4 Bird Islands to the north-west-by-north. The easterly islands may have been the Sir Charles Hardy Islands, fifteen miles away and rising to 320 feet.

5 The dogfish is a small shark of the family *Squalidae*, usually found in cooler waters. In this context, following Beaglehole, *Cook's Journal*, Vol. 1 p. 394, it may be *Scyliorhinus* sp. 'Squibs' reads 'squids' in the log.

6 Sunday Island is at 11°56'S, 143° 13'E. Bligh is again two minutes of latitude too far south; the error in longitude has not changed significantly, the course since Restoration Island having involved only small amounts of westing.

Cannoe ab.[t] 33 feet long bottom up made of three pieces with a sharp head a little carved in resemblance of a Fishes head – & three feet wide – I suppose would carry 20 Men[1] –

All the Country is like Dampiers descrip.[n] of it.[2] –

This Isl[d3] of a Moderate height very rocky & only shrubs & wire Grass. The Tide appears to rise here about 4 or 5 feet. – I went on the heights but saw no land more to the North than WbN Several Isl[ds] lay to the E & SE & some NWbN[4]

Parties return.[d] at Noon with some fine Oysters & Clams & Dog Fish – Squibs.[5] –

Began to Cook Dinner

At Noon I found by Good Observation the lat.[d] of this place $11°58$ S.[o] & Long.[d] by Acc.[t] $144°.29'$E.[y6] – A tide or Current has set in our favor 17 Miles North a little Westerly.

[67]

1 Bligh has omitted from his notebook all reference to the most significant event that occurred on Sunday Island, the angry clash between himself and the carpenter, Purcell. The journal makes much of it, as does Fryer in his account, and the episode has been used by both the detractors and supporters of Bligh. According to Bligh the carpenter began to be insolent 'to a high degree', telling his captain that he was as good a man as he. Alarmed lest his authority be compromised, Bligh seized a cutlass and ordered Purcell to take up another and defend himself. The carpenter than called out that Bligh was about to kill him and started to apologise. Only Nelson, the botanist, supported Bligh, Fryer, next in command, deliberately ordering Cole, the boatswain, to put him under arrest. Bligh responded by promising to kill Fryer first if any trouble arose out of his interference. 'This is the outlines', Bligh says in his journal, 'of a tumult which lasted about a quarter of an hour.' Fryer's version has a more probable tone to it. Because not all the men were equally efficient or willing in the gathering of oysters an agreement was made by which three separate groups would keep for themselves all such findings. Bligh, nevertheless, asked Purcell to hand over his oysters when he returned to the boat, and it was this that led to the altercation. Purcell refused to take up the cutlass against his officer. Fryer at this moment came on the scene, and laughed at the sight of Bligh 'swagering with cutlass over the carpenter's head'. The master, not too amused to forget the impropriety of the action, then said, 'no fighting here – I put you both under arrest', which caused Bligh to turn upon him in a fury. After the carpenter had given an acceptable explanation of his remark Bligh asked his pardon and the matter rested. When Bligh later privately chastised Fryer for his behaviour the master said that Bligh, by taking up a weapon, had put himself on the same footing as the carpenter. There were other ways more suitable for exercising authority than the use of force. This was but one of the many unhappy exchanges between the two men; it is abundantly clear from the notebook, the log and from Fryer's account, that Bligh was irritated with his companions for most of the voyage.

2 These pencilled notations appear to have been made at noon, the time to which they refer. It is impossible to tell whether the whole page was still blank at noon, to be completed later, after the sights were taken and worked. See also note 7 below.

3 The peaked mountain was Middle Peak, four miles south-west of the Western corner of Shelburne Bay.

4 These are Bird Islands, twelve miles north-west of Sunday Island.

5 Tenesmus is a painful contraction of the muscles of the lower bowel.

6 The mainland, on this bearing, was fourteen miles distant, and is low undulating country with an occasional hill reaching 200 feet or more. The bearing covers such a hill of 233 feet.

7 These figures are of great interest, being the only reference to the presence aboard of the Ramsden sextant. The 'B' identifies it as the ten-inch instrument mentioned by Bligh before the BOUNTY sailed from England. The simultaneous sight with the quadrant was taken by Fryer, who at last was allowed to perform his professional duty. Bligh's sight is one minute too far south, a trivial matter, but it is interesting to note that the 'old' quadrant was nearly as accurate and did not deserve the opprobrium implied by the constant reference to its age.

H	K	F	Courses	Wind	Rem^s Mond^y June 1st 1789
1				SEbS	Very fine w^r & we sail in charming smooth water[1]
2					
3					
4	4	6	NWbN	"	Sailed at ½ past 3 the Isl^d off the North part of the Main & it on at WbS – Many Birds & Fish – A peeked mountain & dis^t land came open WbS ¼S[3] – Saw land as far as WNW.
5	4	6	RB	55°:56[2]	
6	4	6	Old Q	55 - 56	
				3	

Low water at Noon –

7			At 6 At Lagoon Isl^{ds}.[4] – could not land being a
8			Rocky shore. –
9			Slept in the Boat at a Grapnel.
10			At day light got the Boat in.
11			Parties went in search of Provender found
12			only a few species of the Pea kind or Dollacus.
1			No oysters. – A party went to the East Isl^d. to
2			see if any thing to be got there. –
3			Some of the People sick at the stomach
4			Saw a Mark of Turtle –
5			Obliged to let the Boat lye aground the Tide. –
6			At Noon Fresh Trade SE & Fine W^r. Party
7			return M^r. Nelson sick. Carpenter & several
8			others – Some have been troubled with violent
9			Tenesmusses[5]
10			⚓ [anchored] An Isl^d WbN¼N 4 leag^s. –
11			Main as far as WNW distinct NW coming[6]
12			

R.B.	55.56[7]	55.56	O^d.Q
	13	3	
	56:09	55.53	
	33:51	13	
	22.4	56.06	
	11.47	33.54	
		22.4	
	Old Quad^t. =	11.50	

[68]

1 These comments refer to the events of 1 June.

2 Hannibal Islands, of 40 feet and 50 feet in height.

3 Mangrove oyster (*Saccostrea commercialis*), one of the food chain associated with mangrove swamps.

4 In the journal Bligh says the sufferers 'had gorged themselves with a large quantity of undressed Beans', although Nelson suggested that some might really have been poisoned by the berries they had eaten.
See note 4, page [59], 29 May.

Rem^s.[1]

High water 3^h. flows 5 feet – Flood from the South^d. as near as I could observe it. –

At 1 I went to the Top of the Isl^d. saw two Keys in the NWbN[2] but no continent farther than I saw before. –

At 2 Dined sumptuously & at 3 I sailed for the Keys in the NWbN expecting to get some Turtle. – We are all vastly recruited by our shell fish dinners. –

Found a kind of Pea that grows on the ground on vines species of the Dollacus.

These oysters grow on the Rocks & are blackish & resemble the Mangrove Oyster[3] – They are very difficult to open or get off the Rocks reason could get no more This Isl^d. is mostly surrounded by Rocks – In some places Sandy Bay – Fish in the Lagoon. The one we are on is the West^{ly}. Key of Three that form this Lagoon – Another Rocky Key lies to the SW & a small Sandy one near it – Toa Tree the leaf of wch. is like a Fir is here & many other Tropical Bushes. The Fine Oysters we met with at last Isl^d. are none here. –

People who are sick attribute their illness to eating of the Dollacus, but I believe it is owing to their Berries & to voraciously[4]

[69]

of what we have had for I could not prevent them – for my own part I am thank God very well & much recruited in strength.

No sign of any Quadruped

Picked up a full grown cocoanutt shell & saw part of a Wigwam – and two Backs of Turtle. –

Picked up 3 Birds Eggs 2 had young ones & other good. –

All the Rocks are a light kind of Stone & in some places very Sharp & bad walking on them.

Dined on ½ our days allowance of Bread oysters & clams we brought from Sunday Isl^d. & thickened with the Dollacus – Some would not eat the Pease but others & myself did. – I think they are good – Some dryed ones were found & eat by those who were ill, they were hard & flinty. – M^r. Nelson found a burning in his Bowels, loss of sight & great drought but no feaver – Incapacity to walk. –

Party got only a few Clams at East Key. Birds innumerable of the Noddy Kind –

[70]

1 This is another account of the noon sight taken with the sextant and the quadrant. The longitude error is the result of Bligh's belief that he is abeam of Cape York, for which he has a position in Hamilton Moore. In fact he is the victim of two errors, the cape not being Cape York and the position available for him for that cape being greatly in error. See the note to the calculations for 2 June.

2 'A kind of chisel thought to have been favoured by the islanders', according to Bowker.

Low Water at Noon
High at 5 ½ follg after

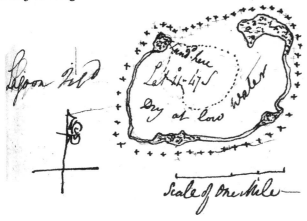

[Sketch map of Bird Islands (Bligh's Lagoon Islands)]

Lat^d Obs^d on the Westerm^t Isle by $\Big\}$ 11°:47'S
     Rams^d B^r
By Common Quad^t 11:50S
Long^d by Acc^t 144"24'E
           Error   3:5
                141:19

All the Main to be seen from here showes in Hills & low land with many
Sand Hills –
Left some Toeys[2] & Gilt Buttons on a Tree tied to a branch. –

[71]

1 This is the only reference in the notebook to the celebrated 'bushfire'
   caused on the island, according to Bligh, by Fryer's disobedience of orders.
   Again, Fryer's account is different and phrased in a manner that is critical of
   Bligh. Bligh was justifiably worried that the blaze might attract natives from
   the mainland, against whom they would be helpless.

2 This word lost in the binding.

3 They sailed at 6 a.m.

4 A variation of 'ye', the conventional method of writing the definite article
   until about the middle of the eighteenth century; $\frac{e}{y}$ was the form mostly
   employed by mariners, who, like Bligh, continued to use this form until about
   the end of the century. I am indebted to Associate-Professor Norman Talbot,
   of the University of Newcastle, for this information.

5 It is difficult to plot the precise track of the launch during its passage from
   Bird Islands to Turtle Island, particularly as some of Bligh's remarks are
   influenced by his mistaken identification of a cape as Cape York, prompted by
   the wrong latitude for Cape York given in Hamilton Moore, who placed it 35
   miles too far south. Bligh's bearings and comments would suggest that he
   thought Orfordness was Cape York, but other remarks would be more appropriate to False Orfordness, some miles to the south. Captain Douglas Wood,
   a B.H.P. master with considerable experience of this region, feels that the
   reference to a cape, particularly a high cape, must be to False Orfordness,
   and not Orfordness, further north.

H	K	F	Courses	Wind	Rem.s Tuesd.y June 2.d 1789
1					Strong Gales & Squally some Slight Showers. –
2					
3	"	" "	"		Boat floated but too Windy to proceed I
4					therefore determined to stay until morning &
5					give the People rest by a good fire on shore[1]. –
6					Boiled some Clams for tomorrow dinner & by
7					issuing a little wine I have saved & bread
8					M.r Nelson got restored & also the Carpenter
9					who suffered great Agony as several have
10					done by the severe Tenesmuss. –
11					
12					
1	"	" "	"		A Party went to look for Turtle & another
					to catch Birds of the latter only 12 were
					Caught. Noddies & [ ][2] innumerable.
2					
3					
4					
5	"	" "	"		Sick People better got in the Boat & sailed.[3] –
6					
7	4	6	NNW	SE.ly	Much Sea at an opening in Reef. – Soon after
					came upon Extensive reef pass.d a sandy Spot.
					An Isl.d N ½ E 3 leag.s Two others were 4 Miles
					& North.n land insight NW 6 leag.s – Clear
					water in shore, and smoother water.
8	5	"	NbW	"	
9	5	"	56.15		
10	5		13		
11	5		28		A Sandy I.d true East 3 m.s and is ab.t 4 leag.s or
					5 from c/y[4] Main
12	4	4	33.32		At Noon an Isl.d NE 2 M.s a sandy spit E
			22:14		3 miles An Isl.d over it EbN ½ N 6 Miles. Cape
			11:18S.o	York WbS 3 leag. S.o most Land S ½ E
					North.n Land NW ½ N 6 leag.s & a Sandy Isl.d
					West 4 Miles – Main Sandy Hills.[5] –

[72]

1 These comments refer to events of Tuesday, 2 June.

2 This was Peckover's watch, appropriated by Bligh.

3 Presumably the Pudding Pan Hill of the modern chart, five miles north-west of False Orfordness.

4 Possibly Shadwell Point and Tern Islet.

At day dawn¹ sailed – Found my watch stoped² – I must now guess at the hour of the day wch must be imperfect as to time of events. – Passed the North^n Land seen from Lagoon Isl^d WNW & NW about 3 or 4 leagues off. – All $^e/_y$ Main continues of a moderate height & full of Sand Hills. – The alteration of the Sea induces one to think we have passed several openings to the Sea through the Reefs –

My Lat^d Cape York (if it is the Cape) is 11°.18S. It is a Sandy Cape Spotted with what grows on it – A long Sandy Isl^d just above water lies to the North^d & eastward of it & bore West of us at Noon – on the Main a few leag^s to the north^d are two remarkable Hills which we called the Paps. Com^g from $^e/_y$ South^d C. York may be first known by a flat Hill at the back of it wch resembles a pudding Pan turned upside Down³. – The northmost land in sight terminated in a low point & a key bore NEbE ab^t 3 or 4 Leag^{s}⁴

The Isl^d NE 2 Miles is a pretty spot full of trees & lies easterly of the low point 4 or 5 leagues. –

[73]

[The following original page is blank, the folded sheet bearing the original 'Eye sketch of part of New Holland' being glued to it.]

1 This sketch map appears to be the original from which the map facing
   p. 220 in Bligh's *A Voyage to the South Sea*, London, 1792, was drawn. With
   some imagination both maps could be seen as supporting the claims of
   Orfordness to be the cape mistaken by Bligh for Cape York.

Eye Sketch of Part of New Holland in the Bounty's Launch by Lieu! Wm Bligh[1]

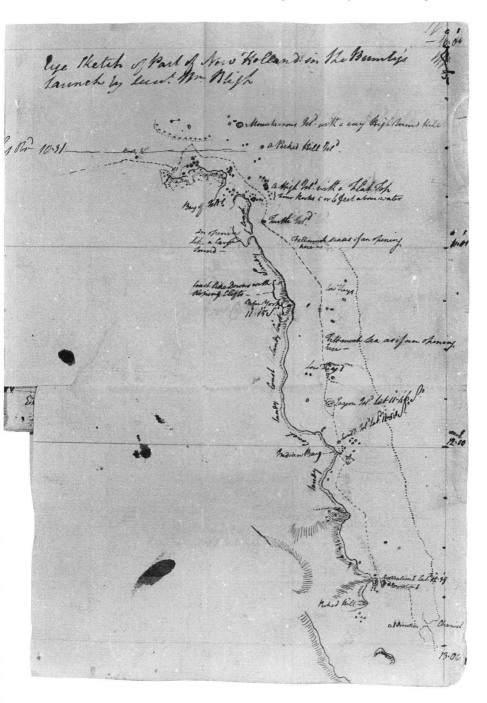

1 Perhaps the red cliffs south of Usher Point.

2 This refers to the cape wrongly identified as Cape York.

3 The entrance to the Escape River.

4 The manuscript has only the symbol for 'anchored'.

5 Turtle Island.

6 Mount Adolphus Island.

7 Adolphus Channel.

8 The word, possibly 'islet', is missing in the manuscript.

9 'Seven' here is really an editorial guess. The reef is North-West Reef, the northern boundary of Prince of Wales Channel, the main channel used by modern shipping. Bligh had missed Endeavour Strait, to the south.

10 Ince Point.

11 Western extremity of Goods Island.

12 'LL' refers to the 'lower limb' of the sun, his normal method. Bligh's longitude from Tofua, after correcting for the initial error, is 67 minutes too far east.

H	K	F	Courses	Wind	Rem.^{s} Wed.^{y} June 3. 1789
1	4	4	NbW	SEbS	Fine W.^{r} A Clift Head bore true West dis.^{t} 4 leag.^{s}[1] – Dined on some boiled Clams & usual allow.^{n} of Bread & Water
2	5	4			
3	4	4			
4	5	″	NW		At 4.^{h}C. York True S.^{o} 6 or 7 leag.^{s}[2] & north.^{n} land in sight NWbW
5	5	″			At 5 abreast of an extensive inlet bear.^{g} SWbS 7 or 8 Miles[3]
6	4			SSE	At ¼ before 6 ⏄ [anchored][4] in 8 feet off an Isl.^{d}[5] 6 Miles from the Main – A High Isl.^{d}
7					NbW 4 leag.^{s}[6] & the Main from NNW½W 5
8					leag.^{s} to SEbS 6 leag.^{s} – Fresh Gales &
9					Cloudy W.^{r}
10					
11					
12					
1					
2					
3					
4					
5					½ past Sailed
6	2	″	NbW	SEbS	
7	5	″			At 8 stand.^{g} between the Isl.^{d} at NbW last night & several others towards the Main.[7] No Ground at 12 fm.^{s} dis.^{n} across 3 Miles
8	5	″	NNW		
9	5	″	NWbW	SEbE	
10	5	2			At 9^h Land as far as NW½W at ½ past 10 a small Rocky [ ][8] true East 2 M.^{s} & another WNW 4 M.^{s}
11	5	4	NW	SEbS	
12	4		SW	SSE	At Noon Isl.^{ds} from NWbW 5 leag.^{s} to NE
	1	4			5 Leag.^{s} – Seven Reef[9] from West to NE Wednes.^{d} Isl.^{d} N.^{o} point EbS 5 Miles[10] West Land in sight SW 7 Miles[11]

Lat Obs.^{d} 10°:31′S Mer.^{d} Alt LL56:54[12]

[76]

1 Bligh is still confused over Cape York.

2 The point is probably Fly Point. The islands are Albany Island, Mount Adolphus Island, Little Adolphus Island and the surrounding rocks.

1 This was, in fact, the entrance to Endeavour Strait, for which Bligh was searching but did not recognise. He now took a broad curving track north-west around the top of Wednesday Island, to enter Prince of Wales Channel. He continued to compare his actual surroundings with his recollection of Cook's description, but naturally could not reconcile them.

2 Perhaps Moa and Badu Islands and the nearer Hawkesbury and West Islands.

This Clift Head is perhaps C. York as it agrees exactly with the lat.[1] – If so it may be known by the Paps lying at the back of it & a few reddish Sand Hills near it – All the others are white sand

At 2 Little or no wood on the Coast & the North.ⁿ land in sight tapering to a point with some Hillocks on it –

Apparently in Sound.ᵍˢ More see & every thing indicating less sheltered by any Reef to the Es.ᵈ/w. A few miles of land now abreast of us looks like Downs with high sloping Clifts to the Sea. –

I brought to for the night being Windy – Went on shore found signs of the Natives having been here Turtling – Isl.ᵈ 1 ½ round rocky all round except a point at the SW End were we lay. –

From the Hillock Point formed a deep Bay & Inlet – Ab.ᵗ 6 Miles further North opposite the Isl.ᵈ the land very low & covered with white Sand for 6 Miles further north, it then gets higher towards p.ᵗ Possession or what I take to be such off[2] which lie sv.ᴵ Islands the north.ᵗ the highest and to the east of which lie 4 high Rock[s] much like each other. – Wood in most places. but apparently barren in other respects. – Other Isl.ᵈ lie to the NNW of high Isl.ᵈ – No Sand Hills – Rocky as I advanced towards the NW the Main in the

[77]

SW appeared as a Parcel of High Islands which might from the appearance of it be called the Bay of Islands.[1] But I believe they may all join by low land. – More land was now seen ahead and small Keys to the NW taking that direction as if the Boundary of the reef was Such – The Country now seems to be Rocky & no Sand Hills

At 11 the Main appeared to be broken & formed deep Inlets & Isl.ᵈˢ – Isl.ᵈˢ more considerable than what we have seen & some very high appeared in the N & NW[2] – The whole seems a wonderfull place – I do not imagine that any of the Isl.ᵈˢ are joined by Reefs, if I may judge from those I've seen and now pass several between me & the Main, & others are constantly appearing. –

At Noon discovered a Reef extendg from West to NE whether this reef joins round to the S.ᵈ I cannot say or whether it is connected to some more to the North – Some small Keys, I could just see in the Range of the Reef & therefore perhaps the High Isl.ᵈ to the North.ᵈ are not connected with it. –

[78]

1 Booby Island, similarly named by Cook in 1770. In the journal Bligh shows he
   is aware that it is the same island as seen by Cook.

2 South-west tip of Prince of Wales Island to northern edge of Hammond Island.

H	K	F	Courses	Wind	Rem.^s Thursd.^y 4 June 1789

H	K	F	Courses	Wind	Rem.ˢ Thursdʸ 4 June 1789
1	3		WSW	SSE	Fair W.ʳ Dined on 6 Oysters &
2	3		"	"	Came into Shoal Water Sand Banks
3	3	4			
4	3	4	"	"	West Isl.ᵈ North 3 or 4 leag.ˢ a Key West ½S 2 leag.ˢ Extrem.ʸ of the Isl.ᵈˢ & Main from EbN 5 leag.ˢ to SE½E 2 leag.ˢ – Course made good to 4 WSW
5	4	4			
6	4	4			At 5½ at the Key w.ᶜʰ¹ I found to be a barren Rock. West part Main ESE & EbN the East part²
7	4	6			
8	4	6		SE	
9	4	6			
10	5				
11	5				
12	5			"	Fresh Gale
1	5	6			
2	5	2			
3	4	6			
4	4	4			
5	5	2		ESE	
6	5	4			A cross going Sea shipt much water – clear Sea & deep Water
7	5				
8	4	4			
9	5				
10	5				
11	5				
12	4	6			Fair W.ʳ – Dined on 6 oysters & Bread

113

Lat. Obs.ᵈ 10.48

[80]

1 These remarks refer to Thursday 4 June.

2 Probably influenced by his recollection of Cook's journal; see above.

After seeing the Reef¹ I kept now in shore to the SSW; SW & W^{ly} Came into shoal water – Several Sandy Banks breaking. Stood round them to the North^d & steered WbS. At 4 another Key appeared West. – I computed the Mean Course from the bear^{gs} of the Land as far as 4 O'Clock. –

Steered for the Key & found it a barren Rock & bold to – having fair Sea I steered on WSW not being able to Steer across heavy seas if the Wind comes South. –

Towards Morning found a high Sea run^g at Noon Fair W^r

The Key is an entire Rock & the resort of Boobies. I therefore calld it Booby Key²

[81]

1 There are 35 varieties of sea-snakes in Australian waters, of which the
   most wide-ranging is the yellow-bellied *Pelamis platurus*. (*The Australian
   Encyclopaedia*, Sydney 1983, vol. 9, p. 102.) Since the yellow-bellied variety
   has black blotches on its tail, it is probably the subject of Bligh's description.

2 The porpoise is a small cetacean, up to two metres, with a blunt, rounded
   snout. The name is used interchangeably with that of the dolphin (not the
   fish), a two-to-four metre cetacean with a well-defined beak and a differently
   shaped dorsal fin.

H	K	F	Courses	Wind	Rem.⁵ Frid.ʸ 5 June 1789
1	4	4	W½S	ESE	Fair W.ʳ & less Sea
2	4	4			All hands as well as can be expected but very weak
3	4	6			Passed 5 snakes – Yellow & spotted black & dark brown¹
4	3	4			
5	3	6			
6	4	4	"	"	
7	4				Saw Porpoises² – Water as usual for Supper – People wanted Bread.
8	4				
9	4				
10	4				
11	4				
12	4				
1	4	4			Showers of Rain
2	4	4			
3	4	4			
4	4	4			
5	4	4			
6	4	4	"	"	Fair W.ʳ & Strong Trade
7	5				
8	5				
9	5				
10	5		West	EbS	Saw some Snakes & Sea Weed – Flying Fish.
11	5	4			
12	5	4			D.ᵒ W.ʳ Bread & a little dryed Dog Fish for Dinner

108

Lat. Obs.ᵈ 10°45′S

[82]

H	K	F	Courses	Wind	Rem.ˢ Saturd.ʸ 6 June 1789
1	4	5	WbN	EbS	Fine W.ʳ and Ship but little Water. – Fresh Trade
2	4	5			
3	4	5	"	"	People complaining of Weakness
4	4	6			
5	5	4			
6	5	4		"	Caught a Booby & as before some of us ravenous for even the Blood
7	5				
8	5				
9	5				
10	5				
11	5				
12	5				
1	5		" "	"	
2	5				
3	5				
4	5			SE	
5	5		"	"	Cloudy & Showers.
6	5				
7	5				
8	5				Theft of Clams committed
9	5				Saw a Gannet & a Sand Lark – Some Snakes
10	4	4			
11	4	4		ESE	
12	5				

119

Lat.ᵈ Obs.ᵈ 10°19′S D.º W.ʳ Fair Intervals
Dined on the Booby and an allow.ⁿ of bread.

[84]

1 This is the start of an anxious period for Bligh, who is worried that he might miss Timor. The references in the *Tables Requisite* to Timor are to 'Timor (W. Point)', 10° 23'S, 123° 59' E, and 'Timorland (S. Point)', 8° 15'S, 131° 54'E. The first position was accurate for latitude and only half a degree of longitude too far east. The second position refers in fact to the Tanimbar Islands, some 240 miles east of the north-east tip of Timor. The longitude in this case was 70 minutes too far east for the southern tip of the Tanimbar Islands. Hamilton Moore was more confusing, the 9° S latitude given for the north end of Timor being 30 minutes too far south. The longitude for Timor at 9° S is 26° 05'E, or nearly two degrees west of that given by Moore. Even if the actual northern end of Timor is taken, Moore's figure is still 40 minutes too far to the east. Moore also listed the west point of Timor at 10° 30'S, 122° 55' E; the latitude is reasonable and the longitude is only 35 minutes or so too far west. His position for 'Timorland' was however totally confusing and would in fact place it on the western side of Timor.

2 This was to avoid passing south of Timor.

3 Bligh found that he had nineteen days allowance of bread left at the former daily ration of one-eighth of a pound, two ounces, to which he now reverted, issuing bread again for supper.

H	K	F	Courses	Wind	Rem.ˢ Sund.ʸ 7 June 1789
1	4	2	WNW	ESE	Fresh Breeze & Trades
2	3	6	NW½W		Examined the Bread & found 19 days
					allowance at ⅛ of a lb per Man. –
3	3	6	"	"	
4	3	6	"	"	Requisite Tables lies E.ⁿ part of Timor – in
					131° 54′E Hamilton Moor – 128°00ᴵ –
5	3	6	"	"	
6	4	4	"	"	
7	4	3			Hauled to the north.ᵈ for fear of a lee current²
8	5	2	NW	SE	
9	5	2			
10	5	2			
11	5				I now gave Bread & water for hoping for
					Supplies at Timor³
12	5				
1	5	2			
2	5	2	NW½W		
3	5				
4	5				
5	5				
6	5				
7	5		WNW	ESE	Squally W.ʳ & much Sea from SE. – Bread &
					Water for Breakf.ᵗ
8	5				
9	5	4	W½S	–	Tropic Gull & Sheerwaters Flying Fish –
10	4	4			
11	5				
12	4	4	"	"	D.ᵒ W.ʳ obs.ᵈ Lat.ᵈ 9° 31′S.ᵒ
					Dined on bread and Water We now anxiously
					pray to make the land

[85]

1 The surgeon, Ledward, and Lebogue were failing rapidly; Bligh tried to help
   them with a teaspoonful or two of wine at daylight.

H	K	F	Courses	Wind	Rem.^s Mond.^y 8 June 1789
1	5	"	WNW	East	Fresh Gales & Squally & threat.^g bad w.^r – Begin to ship much water & people become less & less able to bear it.¹
2	5	"			
3	5	"			
4	5	"			
5	5	"			
6	5	"			Tropic Gulls Mother Carey & some Sheerwater.
7	4				
8	4				Bread & water for Supper
9	4				
10	4				
11	4				
12	4			ESE	
1	5	3			
2	5				
3	4	4		E	
4	5				
5	4	4			
6	4	4		ESE	Mod & Cloudy. Long Sea from ESE.
7	4				
8	4				
9	3	4		ENE	Squally with showers Bread & water for Breakf.^t
10	4			E.^l	Saw a Gannet Tropic Gulls & Flying Fish
11	4			EbS	
12	3			ESE	Bread & Water for Dinner
	106				Fair W.^r & Showers Obs.^d Lat.^d 8°45′S.^o

[86]

1 'Dolphin' refers to a fish of the genus *Coryphaena*, which is fast-swimming, brightly coloured and excellent eating. It can grow up to almost two metres. (*The Australian Encyclopaedia*, Sydney, 1983, Vol. 3, p. 217.)

2 See note above on Timor positions. Bligh seems to have combined the two authorities with respect to the latitude span of Timor.

H	K	F	Courses	Wind	Rem^s Tuesd^y 9th. June 1789
1	3	4	WbS½S	ENE	Mod. & Fair – Some Showers
2	4	2		d^o.	
3	4		WbS		
4	3	4		SE	
5	4	2			Caught a Dolphin^1 wch. rejoiced us – Served ab^t. 2 oz of Offals & others Raw – wch. was a happy relief to us – Hung up the rest to dry for tomorrow – I take the Lat^d. of 9° 00′S^o. to strike Timor in Acc^d to H. Moore
6	4	2	SEbS		New Seamen's Ass^t lays Timor from 10° 30′S to 8° 15^2
7	4	"			
8	4	"			
9	4	4			
10	4	2			
11	4	2			
12	4	2			
1	5				
2	5				
3	5				
4	5				
5	5				
6	5			SE	Men of War Birds Tropic Gulls & a Gannet seen
7	5				Bread & Water for breakf^t.
8	5				
9	4	4			Saw a Booby
10	5				
11	4	4		SEbE	
12	5				Fair W^r. Bread & 1 oz of Fish per Man –
	109				Obs^d. Lat^d. 9°10′S^o. –

[88]

1 These are Moore's figures for the north end of Timor.

H	K	F	Courses	Wind	Rem.ˢ Wed.ʸ 10 June
1	5		W½S	SEbE	Fine W.ͬ
2	5				
3	5				Saw a Gannet a Booby
4	4	2			Many Gull Kind – Flying Fish. –
5	4	2			
6	4	4	"	"	Served Bread & Water for Supper
7	4	4			
8	4	4			9.0 – 128.0¹
9	4	6			
10	5				
11	5				
12	5				
1	4			ESE	
2	4				
3	4				
4	4				
5	4	4			Fair W.ͬ Gannet Man of War Birds – Porpoises. –
6	4	4			
7	5				
8	4	4			Many Sea Fowl Fish Boobies & Gannets –
9	4	6			Served Bread for Breakf.ͭ & W [ater]
10	4	4			
11	4	4			
12	4	4			
	111				Strong Trade Served Bread & Dolphin 1 oz for Dinner

Obs.ᵈ 9°16'S

[89]

1 The longitude problem again appears; Bligh has been gravely concerned for the past two or three days over the condition of his men, more than half of whom he describes on 10 June as facing 'an approaching end to their distress'. He knows from the rock weed floating past that he is near land but is not sure whether it is Timor or the 'long string of Islands (that) stretch to the Eastward from Timor towards New Guinea, I however hope to fall in with Timor every hour, or else I have scarce a hope but I shall lose some of my People.' He told those people at noon on 11 June that if the east end of Timor was at 128°E the launch was then only ninety-nine miles from it, news that caused 'universal joy and satisfaction'. It is of interest to consider his actual position at that time, when his DR longitude, with its mistaken correction for Cape York, was 126° 45'E. His actual position was probably 126° 25'E. The compounding of errors had strangely produced a result not too much in error. In fact, Bligh 'lost' over two degrees of longitude between Torres Strait and Timor, which had more than compensated for the one and a half degrees of westerly error created by his 'Cape York' correction. He was in fact at noon on 11 June about thirty miles closer to Timor than he believed. In 1792, while following the same route in the PROVIDENCE, Bligh again lost nearly two and a half degrees of longitude, the result of a westerly current.

2 Bligh compares his DR position for noon 11 June with Hamilton Moore's position for North Timor. The difference of longitude in minutes of arc he incorrectly labels miles, an uncharacteristic error which perhaps is an indication of his deteriorating condition, which is mentioned elsewhere on this day. For practical purposes the error of two nautical miles was irrelevant.

1 This is the result of Moore's misleading latitude of 9° S for the northern part of Timor.

H	K	F	Courses	Wind	Rem.ˢ Thursd.ʸ 11ᵗʰ June 1789
1	4		W½S	SE	Strong Trade & fair W.ʳ Much Sea –
2	4				Several Gannets & Boobys & Fish. –
3	3	6			
4	4		″		
5	4	6	″	″	We are now anxious to see the land my reck.ᵍ being nearly up by H. Moore.[1]
6	4	4	″	″	
7	4	2	Reck.ᵍ	up	People very weak. –
8	4	2	WbS		Served Bread & Water for Supper. – No appearance of Land. –
9	4	4			
10	4	6			
11	4	4			9.0 – 128.0
12	5	″			9.41 – 129.50
1	5	″			1.50
2	5				60
3	4	4			110 miles[2]
4	4	4		SSE	
5	4	4			
6	4	4	″	″	Gannet but no sight of Land
7	4	4			
8	4	4	″	″	Several pieces of Rock Weed
9	4				Pleasant W.ʳ – Served Bread & Water. –
10	3	6			
11	4				
12	3	6	″	″	Fine W.ʳ & Less Sea Very Hazy No signs
	107				Land – Bread & Water

Lat Obs 9°41′S 9°24′DR. Distressed.

Bad steerage –

[90]

I steered southerly lest the North part of Timor not being in 9° 00′ I might from a small error in my course pass it altogether[1]

[The calculations which form the rest of the original material on this page will be found with the navigational notes for 11, 12 and 13 June.]

[91]

1 Bligh's calculations of the length of the voyage from Tofua.

2 This is a calculation of the average daily run of the launch obtained by
  dividing the number of days into the distance given by the log. Although the
  figure is obscure in the original it must be 3618, since the journal entry for 12
  June mentions 41 days and 3623 miles. The arithmetical error made by Bligh,
  the most meticulous of people, reveals the effect upon him of the long launch
  voyage, particularly marked during the week before reaching Timor.

H	K	F	Courses	Wind	Rem.ˢ Frid.ʸ 12 June 1789
1	4		W¹/₂S	SEbS	Fine W.ᵗ & Hazy anxiously hope for Timor – Very weak & distressed. –
2	4		"		
3	4		"	SE	
4	4		"	"	Gannetts –
5	4		West	"	Many Gulls Served Bread & Water for Supper
6	4		"	"	No appearance of Land
7	4	4		East	Caught a Booby by hand
8	4	6			
9	5				At 3 saw Timor WNW to WSW
10	5		29 Days May¹		
11	4	4	12		At Day Break Timor NE¹/₂N 7 leag.ˢ to SWbS low land 2 leag. Bore away. –
			41		
12	5				
1	5				
2	5				
3	4	6			At 7 Land opened with the low land at SW
4	3		NNE		At 8 the extremes of Timor from SWbW 5 leag.ˢ to NEbN 6 leag.ˢ & p.ᵗ of low land set at day break NbW 3 Miles –
5	3				
6	3		" SbE	EbS	
7	3		" SbW		
8	3		" SSW		At Ab.ᵗ 10.ʰ High land came open w.ᵗʰ the S.ᵒ extr. as set at 8.ʰ – SW¹/₂W & soon after other land in the same direction.
9	3		" "		
10	3		" "		
11	3		" SWbS	SE	
12	3				At Noon the Low Land Seen at day break NNE¹/₂E 4 leag.ˢ & is the East part seen The S.ᵒ extreme set at 8.ʰ NbE¹/₂E 3 Miles & the S.ᵒ most land in sight SW¹/₂W 5 leag.ˢ
	Lat Obs.ᵈ 9.59S				Booby & Bread for Dinner 41/ 3618/ 89²

$$41/\ 3618/\ 89^2$$
$$328$$
$$\overline{438}$$

[92]

1 These remarks refer to Friday 12 June.

2 In the journal Bligh says he 'had a presentiment that it [the Dutch settlement] was on the S.W. part. I therefore steered to the Southward'.

At Day Light[1] I fetched in with lowland which formed the SE.ⁿ part of
the Isl.ᵈ – It was woody near the shore & other parts bear. An opening
like a Harbour appeared bear.ᵍ West ab.ᵗ 5 Miles to the NW of which
appeared a cultivated Country & from the arrangement of the Trees on
one part it looked like a Gentlemans Seat. A Great sea sat on the shore
and were only 5 Miles from it I therefore hauled out on a Wind to clear
the SE.ⁿ p.ᵗ ab.ᵗ 2 leag.ˢ – I would have put into this apparent Port but I
feared it might be difficult for me to get out again.
Interior parts Mountainous & Woody
Appeared the mouth of a River at the point of lowland – 10.ʰ
Mountains pleasantly diversified by cleared Spots w.ᶜʰ we take to be
cultivated. See no Houses or Smokes. The Extrem.ˢ we now see are high
but the shore has been low we have passed hitherto – Plenty of wood.
I intended to have gone on the South Side but I could not get round & I
expect the Gover.ⁿ residence on the SW part.[2]
Many Cultivated Places & Beautiful Situations. – Coast mountains
sloping to the Sea – Much wind
Saw some Houses. – No shelter for Boats. –
Sea from SE.ˡʸ

[93]

1 The foresail would be trimmed so that with the helm alee the launch would come up to the wind only to fall off again on the same tack, thus making little if any headway.

2 The launch was hove-to on the other tack by turning away from and across the wind; she was, in other terms, gybed onto the other tack.

3 A board, in this context of beating to windward, is the distance run between tacks; the legs of a windward course.

H	K	F	Courses	Wind	Rem.ˢ Satd.ʸ 13 June 1789
1	3	6	SW	SEbE	Fair W.ʳ & Mod. Wind.
2	3	6	WSW		
3	3	4	SW		At 4 the South.ˡʸ land WbS 4 Miles – First or SE Cape NE¾E offshore 2 Miles. – Saw dis.ᵗ high land WbS.
4	4	"	WSW	ESE	
5	5	"	WbS	"	
6	5	"	"	"	
7		"	Up SSE		At Sun Down the South.ⁿ point East 5 Ms. – The Western.ᵗ Land
8					WbS½S 6 leag.ˢ offshore 1½ Mile
9		"	Off SSW		At 6 Hove to under the Fores.ˡ ¹ as before
10					
11		"			
12		"			
1					
2		"	d.º		Wore & Hove to head in shore²
3		"	"	"	
4		"	Up NEbN		
5		"	Off NbW Course from 6 pm WbS 9 miles		At day light found I had drift ab.ᵗ 3 leag.ˢ WbS towards the Westernmost land seen last night – Wore & made Sail. – Land opened w.ᵗʰ the West.ⁿ p.ᵗ at West. The Westernm.ᵗ point is I believe the most southerly. –
6		"			
7	4	6	W½S	EbS	
8	4	6			
9	4	4	West	ESE	
10	4	4			At 8 West ext.ᵐ as set at night NW
11	2	4	W½N	SE	2 M.ˢ – outer land W½S – W.ʳ Curr.ᵗ & much Sea.
12	2	4			At 10 Saw Land SW 6 or 7 leag.ˢ to SWbW½W an Isl.ᵈ & another dis.ᵗ SW½S 10 leag.ˢ At Noon no Obs.ⁿ in a Bay – After making a board³ to the North. – Bear.ᵍˢ W.ⁿ p.ᵗ WbS½S 3 leag.ˢ Isl.ᵈˢ as before

[94]

1 These remarks refer to Saturday 13 June.

2 Bligh here has correctly observed the traditional 'shifting agriculture' of
   the Timorese.

1 Bligh thought for a time that the island of Roti, off the southern end of
   Timor, was part of the mainland and he therefore altered course to seaward to
   clear it. According to Fryer, however, it was already evident that it was an
   island and that the boat was being endangered by going out to sea unnecessar-
   ily. Although Fryer mentioned this to Bligh the latter refused to listen; when
   it was clear to him that he had made a mistake he tried to blame Fryer for not
   warning him earlier, a reaction that exasperated the master. Again there are
   two sides to this conflict. Bligh was acting as a prudent seaman so long as he
   thought there was danger of being embayed. The passage back to the shore
   was violent, the sea being rough, and throughout it Bligh, says Fryer, needled
   him as if he blamed him for the mistake. Peckover, the gunner, who had seen
   Timor during Cook's first voyage, was also sure that it was Roti they were
   trying to weather.

2 He could not get a true sea horizon, necessary for the sight.

At 3^1 The Coast began to form into Points from the Hills – First Cape makes distinct to the North^d – Country full of wood
Appearance of Shoal water far from the Shore
At 4^h the shore low towards the shore covered wth Trees & particularly those like the Palm Thatch which were taken for Cocoanutts – The High land now began to terminate & trended West & all the southern part in sight low land as I have mentioned. – The sun being over it prevented my having a good View – Could see but few Cultivated Spots –
Run past the South part in 2 fms. water a low shore & flat – Smokes within of clear^g ground.^{2} Dangerous shore for a ship. – At sun down shortened sail. Thus far having found no Town or Place to land – Expect to find the Residence of the Governor on the West Side which I suppose to be round the West^d land insight which is high – Interior parts very mountainous
I hove too lest I might pass any harbour – in the morng. found I was to the West^d of the low land & shoal water & stood along a high shore to ^{e}/$_y$ West covered wth wood without signs of cultivation. –
Strong Gales & very Hazy – When I saw Isl^{ds} I supposed by my lat it was the S^d most part of Timor I thus am fearfull of being embayed hauled out to the SSW

[95]

to see plainer when they evidently appeared as Isld^s – the South^n the highest & as far as 9 or 10 leag^s^{1} – I therefore stood back to bay that promised shelter & every one was solicitous & clamorous to get into to get food, particularly the Master – I found sheltered from the SE only much surf on the shore & after all no one would attempt to land I therefore sailed west^d again & determined not to stop until under the Lee of the Isl^d – or see some Dwelling – lost my observation being too near the Shore^2 – the Country appeared pretty with Lawns & Parks but we found them natural We however saw smokes which I considered to be Malays clearing ground up the Valleys. –
Since on the Coast I have observed places on the Shore like high roads leading into the Country from the Sea Side. – These are said to be Rivers

[96]

1 This is the tide race off the south-west tip of Timor at the entrance to Semau Strait. See Ware's dramatic account of his passage through the same area, *op. cit.* p. 18 and his comments on p. 20.

2 Bligh is moving up Semau Strait.

3 A fort was first constructed at Kupang in 1640 by Portuguese Dominicans defending themselves against the attacks of the Moslem Macassarese. This fort was seized by the Dutch in 1643, but remained isolated until the Dutch defeat of the 'Black Portuguese', or Topasses, in 1749. The real assertion of Dutch power in Timor had to wait, however, until the latter part of the nineteenth century. (J. Jollife, *East Timor, Nationalism and Colonialism,* Brisbane, 1978.)

4 See note at the end of the transcription on the flag patterns sketched on the last page of the original.

H	K	F	Courses	Wind	Rem.^s Sund.^y 14th June 1789
1	4		West	ESE	Strong Gales & Very Hazy a High dangerous Breaking Sea¹
2	4				
3	1		North	"	Steered for between e/y Isl^{ds}. & the Main abreast of wch. An inlet appeared – Steered in & came to a Grapnel on the East side – the Isld.^s SbW¼W to SW½W 5 Leag.^s – West Side of the Bay W½S 2 Mile East point SbW ¾ mile.²
4					Ebb running out –
5					
6					
7					
8					
9					
10					At ½ past 4 Left this place with a Melay
11					Pilot, and kept sailing & rowing with vari.ⁿ
12					airs until ten O'Clock when we came too. –
1					
2					Courses NEbN – NE & NEbE.^y –
3					At 10 'Clock weighed with light airs & not being able to make any land w.^t the sails we pulled along shore NEbE & ENE & East & at
4					dawn came to an ⚓ off the Town of
5					Coupang.³ –
6					
7					
8					
9					Hoisted a Small Jack we made, in the M. Shrouds as in distress⁴ – At 6 I had leave to come on Shore. –
10					
11					
12					At 9 All hands came on shore

At Noon – Boat hauled into the River & every thing out –

[98]

1 These remarks refer to Sunday 14 June.

2 Semau Island lies close to the west of the southern end of Timor, Roti is to the south-west and Sawu, on the southern edge of the Savu Sea, is about 60 nautical miles west of Roti.

3 The journal merely says that Bligh promised to pay the guide for his trouble.

1 'calipee', given in *The Shorter OED* as '(a) the lower shell or plastron of the turtle, (b) that part next the lower shell containing a light yellow gelatinous substance.'

Rem.[1]

A most charming extensive Bay 2 Miles or more across the Entrance and considerably more extensive to the North.[d] and Eastward. – Isld.[s] lye ab.[t] 5 Leag.[s] SSW The Coast lies East and West without. – Whether the Isld.[s] off it is Rotto[2] & Savu I am at a loss to know & I have no Books to tell me & my recollection so bad –

The Land makes in the Bay with mod risings joined by lower Grounds – Saw a Dog & some Cattle on our Shore M.[rs] Peckover & Cole I sent after them.

In Rounding the Bay, along shore the Coast to this place where the land is low it appeared shoalwater & broke in high seas. –

About 4 Party returned with some Melays one of whom agreed to go with me to Coupang w.[ch] I understood was the Governors residence, by showing him a parcel of Dollars.[3] –

All hands overjoyed & in the greatest spirits at this happy appearance of an end to our distress – Got a few heads of Indian Corn –

[99]

& some dryed pieces of callypees[1] of Turtle.

I might perhaps have got some trifles else but as it was clear to me that such an elligible Place for shipping would have some settlement I relyed on the Mellay & went on. –

The Party found a family or two of Mellays – The Women curtseyd & all shewed sign of having connection with Europeans. –

We kept the Eastern side of the bay on board to the NE & ENE – making a true NEbE course nearly I believe dist about 8 miles to where we ⚓ at 10 pm. The Sea was here open to the North & NW & I found I was here at the North Entrance of this Spacious Harbour 1 ½ across While I lay in the South entrance the Ebb Tide run from the North.[d]

[100]

1 A road is a stretch of water near the land where ships may anchor, but which is not sheltered.

& before I left it showed me a reef about 2 Cables length from the East shore where I was which seemed to run in the direction of the shore of this side of the entrance. – A ship must therefore carefully attend to it, as they will see nothing of it at high Water. –

Near the Shores is a flat of shoal water but farther off plenty of depth I have no doubt for any ships. –

In the Middle of this North entrance I sounded 10 fm.ˢ no ground. –

At 1 in the morning we rowed along shore (after making some fruitless attempts with the sails) to the Eastward ENE abᵗ 5 miles.

Saw some Vessels in the Roadᵗ wᶜʰ. gave us most inexpressible pleasure. And a little before day I came to a Grapnel off a Small Town & Fort wᶜʰ. the Pilot told

[101]

me was Coupang. –

At day break I was desired to come on shore by a Soldier who was sent down to the beach & who conducted me to the Fort, but found no person of consequence & the Governor they told me could not be spoke wᵗʰ until 10 O'Clock in the mornᵍ –

Met an English Sailor who belonged to the large Ship in the Road He conducted me to his Captain – Called Spikerman. – This Gentleman behaved with great goodness, & after having told him of my situation I requested care & a situation for my People & officers might be prepared without delay. – He therefore gave the necessary orders for their accomodation and victualling

[102]

for the present but more could not be done untill the Governor who was Ill, permitted any one to visit him. – I now ordered everyone to come on shore which was as much as some of them could being so weak as to be scarce able to walk. – Among these were the Surgeon Mᵣ Ledward, who was reduced to meer skin & bones and Lawrence Lebogue a Seaman equally as bad – those would certainly have died in a few days – Some others were getting ill through a want of resolution and spirits, and all in a very weak condition & scarce able to walk & support themselves. I ranked Among the few of the heartyest ones & was

[103]

1 The title is 'Merchant and Headman of Kupang on the island of Timor. 'Operhoisd' is a misspelling of 'Opperhoofd'.

1 Eighteen men came ashore at Kupang. Nelson died in Timor; Elphinstone, Lenkletter and Hall died soon after reaching the Dutch East Indies; Ledward was lost at sea on the voyage home and Lamb, too, died before reaching England.

Peckover, Cole, Simpson and Purcell returned to England, and Purcell is known to have died in 1834.

Hayward and Hallet sailed again to Tahiti, with Captain Edward Edwards in the PANDORA, in search of the mutineers; both were lost at sea some time later, while serving on other vessels.

Samuels continued in the Royal Navy and rose to Paymaster; Lebogue and Smith sailed to Tahiti again with Bligh in the PROVIDENCE on the second breadfruit voyage. Tinkler and Fryer both served with Bligh at the battle of Copenhagen; Tinkler eventually rose to Post Captain, Fryer served as Master till 1812, and died in 1817.

Bligh ended his naval career with high rank, being appointed Vice-Admiral of the Blue in 1814. He died on 7 December 1817.

certainly the strongest on my Legs but reduced like the others very much & it was favorable to all as I was able to move about & procure the necessary wants. –

At 11 O'Clock I was introduced to the Resident or Governor Wm Adriaan Van Este whose title here is – Koopman en Operhoisd. tot Coepang op het Eyland groot Timor.[1] – This Gentleman shewed himself possessed of every feeling of a humane & good man, he received me with great affection ordered refreshments to be got & a House to be cleared for my use, but under this Roof I was

[104]

obliged to take seamen & Officers or send them to the Hospital or on board of C. Spikⁿ Ship – That this might not be the case I divided the small appartments allotted to me as follows –

one Room I gave to the Master Mr Nelson & Mr Peckover the Gunner & Doctor – another or kind of Loft to the other Officers – Another to the Men, and one I took to myself – a Hall was common to all the officers with a good Piazza round the House & the back part was for the use of the Men. –

Surgeon came to Visit us – Clothes given – Dinner at Noon. –

Mr Nelson & Peckover, Mr Samuels & Hayward only would have lived to have got to Batavia.[1]

[105]

The sketch opposite is of the track from Turtle Island to Booby Rock. The top right calculations are for the difference of latitude between the observed latitudes for 6 and 9 June. Those on the left may be an attempt to calculate the bread ration. The inverted figures, read normally from the top, are the DR longitude for 3 May, the probable difference of longitude between 8 p.m. and noon, 3 May, the approximate longitude of Tofua as estimated by Bligh, the DR longitude 10 May, the difference of longitude between the two previous figures, and that difference converted to minutes.

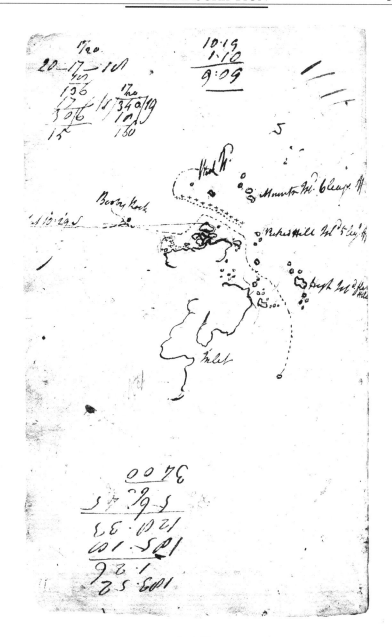

[106]

The sketch represents two attempts to draw the Great Union flag of England and Scotland as it existed until 1800, when the union with Ireland made it necessary to incorporate the red saltire of St. Patrick with the red cross of England and the white saltire of Scotland. The white border around the red cross is the fimbriation denoting the original white ground which is separated from the blue ground of the saltire of St. Andrew. This flag was introduced at the accession of James I for use at sea. It was restricted to the Royal Navy by Charles I in 1634. After a temporary eclipse during the Commonwealth it was restored by Charles II in 1660. (*Encyclopaedia Britannica*, Chicago, 1967, vol. 9, p. 400.) The figures all represent latitude calculations from noon sights for 7, 9, 11, 13, and 18 May, some of which were apparently discarded.

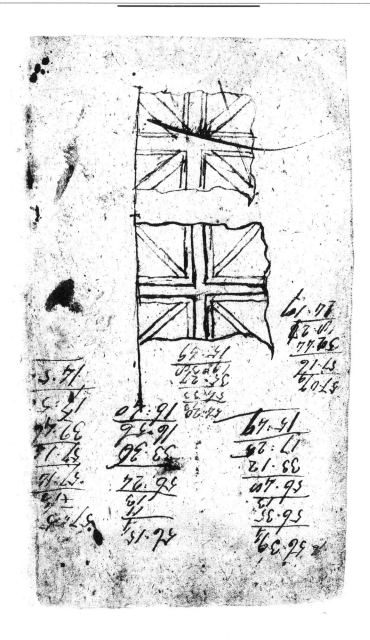

[107]

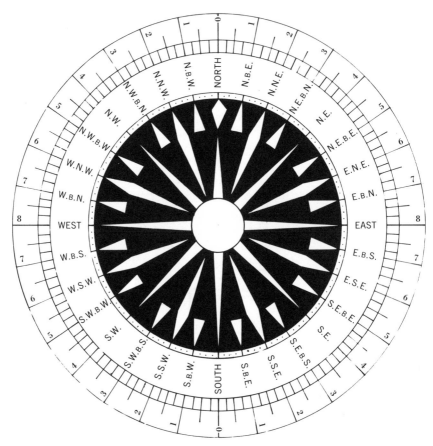

Mariner's compass rose graduated in points rather than degrees, as was the practice as late as the end of the nineteenth century.

THE NAVIGATIONAL CALCULATIONS

As indicated in the Editor's Note, the navigational calculations which appear at intervals throughout the notebook have in this volume been reproduced photographically and placed together at the end of the text, in chronological order. In this way the historical evidence is preserved without editorial tampering, for the benefit of other scholars, a sound historiographical principle. A tidy printed version would, furthermore, fail to communicate to the reader so clearly the idea of the appalling conditions under which the navigational tasks were being performed.

While the Introduction has included a general explanation of the navigational principles employed by Bligh it will still be useful to the reader who seeks completely to understand these calculations to have an idea of the precise procedures involved, together with a detailed account of at least one example.

Bligh, within the limits set by his peculiar circumstances, maintained the normal navigational routine of a Royal Navy vessel, on which the navigational or nautical day ran from noon to noon, and not from midnight to midnight, with the 'day's work' being completed at each noon. This involved the finding of the ship's position from the resolution of all the courses made good and the distances run upon them during the previous twenty-four hours, corrected where possible by actual observations. In Bligh's case these were confined to sun sights, from which his latitude was calculated. He had no means of accurately fixing his longitude.

Aboard ship a log-board, ruled in the same manner as the log-book, was entered each hour with navigational data, including the compass course sailed, the speed in knots and fathoms, the wind direction and, in the larger right-hand space on the page, brief remarks on various relevant matters. At noon these entries were transcribed into the log-book, and the position of the ship recorded. To obtain the DR or 'dead-reckoning' position the change of latitude since the previous noon, as given by the 'northing' or 'southing' made good, and the difference of longitude, obtained by using the mid-latitude of the two noon positions to convert the 'easting' or 'westing' in miles, called 'departure', into minutes of longitude, were applied to the DR position of the previous day. The courses used to obtain these 'resolved' distances were the compass course as entered on the log-board, corrected where necessary for variation and for leeway; in the 'log' pages of the notebook the courses therefore usually appear differently from those in the daily traverse-table calculations.

The above procedure is to be found on each of the daily calculation pages. In addition Bligh frequently worked out the distances and bearings of places, the positions of which were known to him, from his current position. These calculations mention such places as Cape Cumberland in the New Hebrides, Cape York and, of course, his destination, Timor. Where two latitudes and their difference and two longitudes and their difference are seen together, one of these 'distance and bearing' operations is being performed.

In a number of cases a third set of figures is to be found, being the working of a sun sight into a latitude; the figures refer to the sextant sight, the index error when present, the correction for dip, semi-diameter and refraction.

The first two operations, those for resolving the traverse-table and those for obtaining distance and bearing, were performed with the aid of the tables for solving right-angled triangles, usually referred to also as traverse-tables, a source of minor confusion in nomenclature. If a side of the triangle being solved exceeded the 300-mile-limit of the latter tables, it was divided by some figure that would bring it within the range, the other sides having to be similarly reduced. The result, of course, had to be multiplied by the same figure to give a true result, a fact that Bligh on one occasion forgot.

The following annotations will identify briefly the particular navigational operations being performed on each day and will go into detail only when some unusual feature has occurred. One example, nevertheless, that for 22 May, will be described in detail and the curious reader is therefore advised to turn first to that page before perusing the remainder of the annotations and the calculations to which they refer.

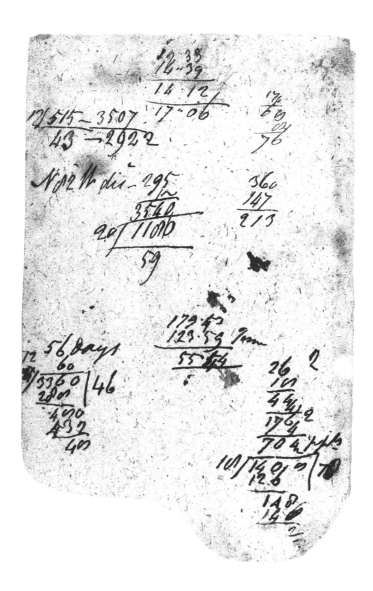

Page 2, undated

These are the most difficult sets of calculations to identify precisely, but in general they are Bligh's early attempts to determine the course and distance to Timor from his position during the first two or three days out from Tofua. His estimate of 1180 leagues and a course of N82°W is close to the actual figures, worked by traverse-tables, of 1196 leages and N81°W. There is also an attempt to estimate the time to reach Timor. The four lines of calculations at the top of the page are concerned with finding the mid-latitude between Bligh's position on 3 May and Cape Cumberland, at the northern end of Espiritu Santo.

Page 4, undated
This page presents several problems. The incomplete corners of the
triangle could mean that the page has been trimmed from a larger size and bound
later into the notebook. It may therefore have been a separate piece of paper in
Bligh's possession, similar to one mentioned in the log on 9 May, on which he
drew a sketch map of New Guinea, New Holland and Timor for the information
of all hands. The triangle is possibly connected with the use of the traverse-
tables. The propositions at the bottom of the page have so far defied precise
interpretation, even by an academic mathematician, although they bear a general

resemblance to the conventions used to describe the properties of triangles. It must be remarked, however, that the entries may have nothing to do with the voyage, since the opposite side of this leaf bears the two entries that were most certainly made retrospectively, probably after Bligh reached Timor, or even England.

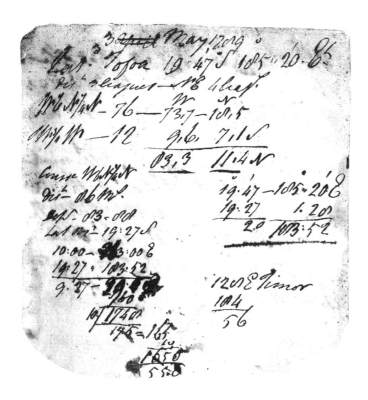

3 May 1789

This is the first of the day's work calculations; in this case the day started at 8 p.m. when the launch 'bore away for Timor' after the escape from the Tongans. The longitude of 213° 00' is interesting, being approximately that of Tahiti, from which Bligh subtracts his DR longitude for this day, 3 May. It suggests that for the moment he is considering the possibility of sailing back to that island, calculated to be 1650 miles away, or 55 days' sail at an average speed of 30 miles daily. This may be the 55 days shown in the calculations on the second page of the notebook, contrasted with the 46 required to reach Timor. It should be noted that the longitude of Tofua is 25 minutes too far east.

4 May

Calculations for the day's work; difference of latitude and longitude between noon position and south-west Timor, as given in *Tables Requisite*; an estimate of the position of the small flat island by resolving its bearing and distance from the launch into minutes of latitude south and minutes of longitude west.

5 May

The day's work; bearing and distance of Cape Cumberland.

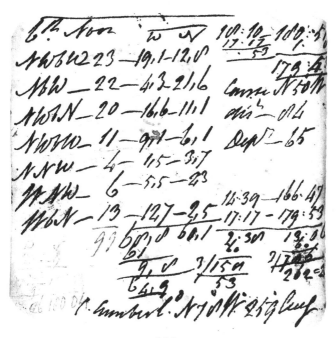

6 May

A good example of the resolution of several courses and distances run being reduced to an 'average' course and distance run for the full twenty-four hours together with the departures or distance made good towards the west. This departure is converted to minutes of longitude, which are subtracted from the longitude of the previous day. The difference of latitude has been found from an observation. Bligh for some reason has applied a negative correction of 3.9 miles to his calculated departure. Also calculations of bearing and distance of Cape Cumberland.

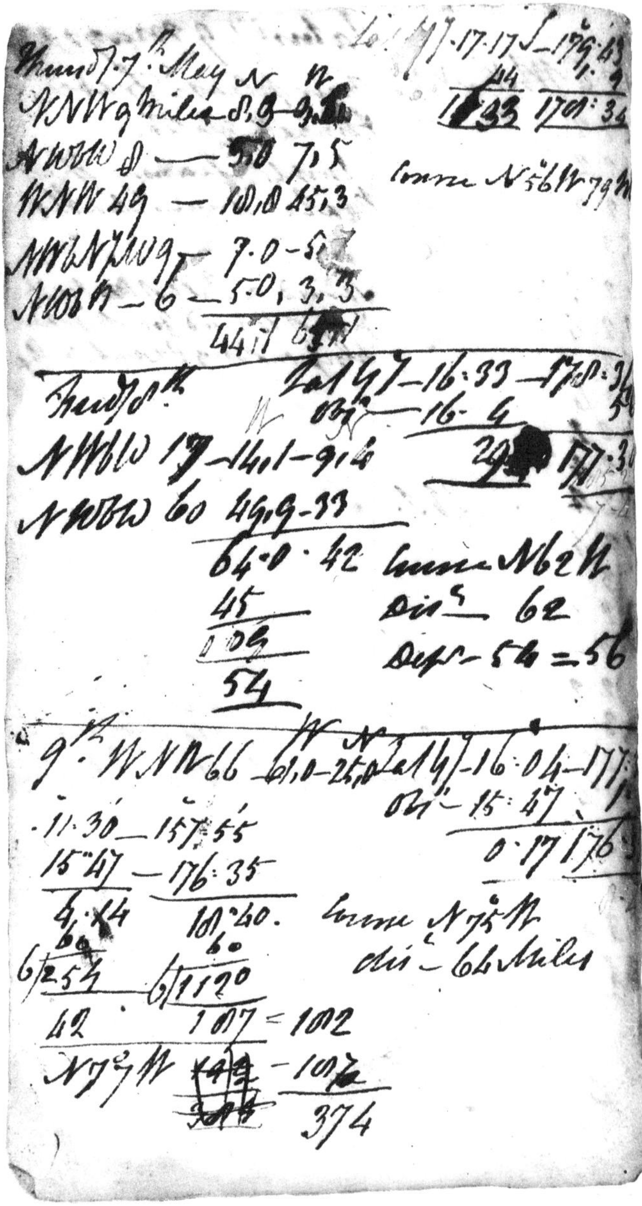

7 May

The day's work; cloud spoiled the noon observation so Bligh has used his calculated northing as the latitude difference. Since the sight he did take was not quite on the meridian he knows that he is at least as far north as that sight showed, that is 16° 40'S.

8 May

The day's work, but with some correction, possibly to compensate for the large difference between the observed difference of latitude and that given by calculation of northing. Bligh has trusted his course steered and his observed latitude although the latter still has to be compared with the uncertain figure for the previous noon. On most of the days from this date until the Barrier Reef was sighted Bligh kept a running total of the longitude he had covered since leaving Tofua. The figure appears immediately below the DR longitude and is entered in pencil.

9 May

The day's work; calculations of bearing and distance of the south-eastern extremity of New Guinea, the northern limit to his desired landfall. The log states 'amused all hands by describing the situation of New Guinea & New Holland and also Timor which I drew on a piece of Paper'.

10 May

The day's work and bearing and distance of Cape Cumberland.

11 May

The day's work.

12 May

The day's work.

13 May

The day's work and bearing and distance of Cape Cumberland.

14 May

The day's work, the several courses being those steered around the Banks Islands; the figures at bottom left are the working of a sun sight to obtain the latitude.

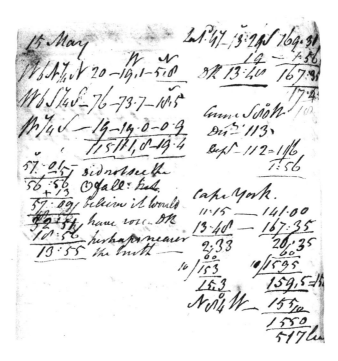

15 May

The day's work; bearing and distance of Cape York (unknown to Bligh this was a futile exercise, since his own position and that of Cape York are both incorrect). The calculations bottom left are for determining the latitude from his observation of the sun, the latter, Bligh notes, likely to have been made before the sun was on the meridian.

16 May

The day's work; bearing and distance of south-eastern New Guinea, although the latitude used here is 15 minutes further north. The log expresses fear of being driven by the southerly winds 'too near New Guinea'.

17 May

The day's work.

18 May

The day's work; no observation used but one apparently made and discarded, probably that shown in the centre of the last page, just below the second flag.

19 May

The day's work; bearing and distance of Cape York, a worked and discarded observation.

20 May

The day's work; sun observation and calculation of latitude.

21 May

The day's work; the distance in a northerly direction to the south-eastern New Guinea position previously mentioned, the distance being simply equal to the difference of latitude. Cape Deliverance was the name given by Bouganville to the south-eastern extremity of New Guinea which he rounded on 26 June 1768 after a most difficult passage to windward along the southern shore of the island, which he had sighted on 10 June after abandoning his attempt to close the coast of New Holland by running down the parallel of 15 degrees south.

22 May

The calculations for this day offer a useful example of all the operations
carried out. The launch has been on three courses, which when converted to
points or fractions of a point north of west are 3/4, 1/2 and 2 1/4 points. (A compass
'point' equals 11°15', one thirty-second of a circle). The tables are opened at
each of these angles in turn and against the distance run on each in the distance
column of the tables there is found in the adjacent columns designated at the
bottom of the page departure and latitude, the westing and northing components.
These total, for all three courses, 129.7 and 17.5. Bligh has obtained an accurate
latitude by observation, which gives him a difference of 12 minutes of latitude
from his previous noon position. He now has two sides of a triangle, the opposite
being the accurate difference of latitude in miles, the adjacent, or departure,
influenced by possible errors in the course and by unknown factors such as
currents. With these two sides he looks in the degrees section of the tables until
they are found in adjacent latitude and departure columns, as shown at the foot
of the page. He accepts 129.5 against 11.3 as being the closest agreement
available, which gives him the third, or distance, side of 130, while the angle at
the bottom of the page on which these figures are found is the course west of
north that he has made good over the twenty-four hours, in this case north
85° west.

The 129.5 miles of departure just found is now converted to minutes of
longitude. To do this the latitude half-way between those of this day and the
previous day is calculated, usually by adding the two latitudes and dividing by
two. This figure is then rounded off to the nearest whole degree and its complement found; in this case the mid-latitude is 14° 23'S, which rounds off to 14°, of
which the complement is 76°. Opening the tables to 76°, Bligh looks for 129.5 in
the departure column and accepts 129 against 133 in the distance column. This
is the change of longitude in minutes, or 2° 13' to the west, which is subtracted
from the longitude of the previous day to give the new DR longitude for 22 May.
Bligh now seeks to find the bearing and distance of Cape York. He first obtains
the difference of latitude and longitude between his position and that of the
Cape, both in minutes. Since the longitude figure is beyond the 300 limit of the
tables he divides both it and the difference of latitude by six. Before proceeding
further with his solution of the triangle the sides must be stated in the same units,
so Bligh now converts the minutes of longitude into miles of departure by
reversing the procedure by which departure had been turned into longitude. The
mid-latitude is again found, being 13° to the nearest degree. Using the headings
at the foot of the page (that is, using the complement of 13°, or 77°) he finds
against the longitude figure of 147 in the distance column the figure of 143.2 in
the departure column. He now has the two sides in the same units, 30 and 143
miles, which, on inspecting the tables, he finds most nearly matched in the
latitude and departure columns of the page opened at 78°. In the third or distance
column is found 147 miles, or one-sixth of the distance between Cape York and
Bligh's position. This is converted to leagues by doubling it, the equivalent of
dividing the full distance by three. The 78°represents the Cape's bearing west
of north from Bligh.

   The figures at the bottom left are the calculation of the latitude from the noon altitude of the sun. An unusually large correction of −6 is applied to the sextant reading, after which the standard combined correction for height of eye, and the sun's semi-diameter and refraction is added. The complement of this corrected altitude, called the zenith distance, is now obtained, and from that figure the declination of the sun, obtained from the tables with a correction for longitude, is subtracted, the result being the latitude of 14° 17'S.

23 May

The same procedures as for the previous day are carried out.

24 May

The day's work and bearing and distance of Cape York.

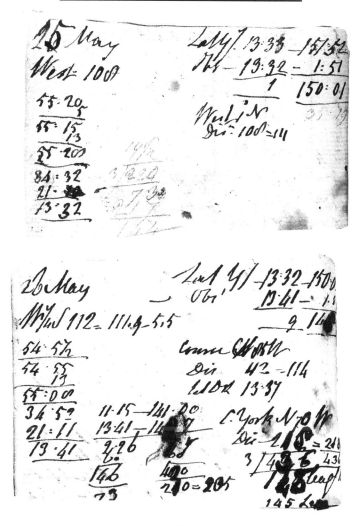

25 May

The day's work and observed latitude calculations. The pencilled calculation to the right of the latitude calculation is Bligh's estimate of the distance in leagues between his estimated position for noon on 26 May and Cape York.

26 May

The day's work; sextant and latitude calculations, bearing and distance of Cape York.

27 May

The same operations as for the previous day.

28 May

The day's work, here made a little more complex by the alterations of course made after sighting the Great Barrier Reef in the early morning; the latitude calculations, a statement of the bearing and distance of Cape York and an estimate of the position of the passage through the reef based on the launch's noon position a little to the north-west of it. The actual position of the passage is 12° 52'S, 143° 50'E. Adventure Bay is in south-eastern Tasmania, where Bligh had been the previous August. His longitude for it as shown here was perhaps taken from Hamilton Moore, who shows it at 147° 31'40" E, or from his own calculation of 147° 33'29"E.

29 May

Calculation of passage to Restoration Island from the Reef. The position is that of Restoration Island found by Bligh.

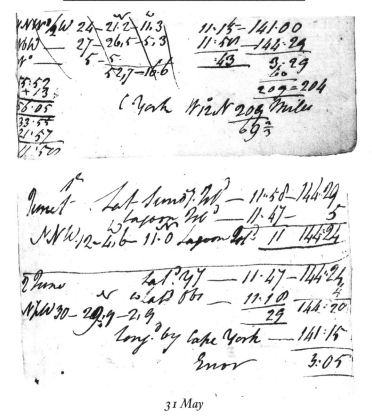

31 May

Calculations for passage from Restoration Island to Sunday Island and position of Sunday Island; latitude calculations and bearing and distance from Cape York.

1 June

The day's work, being passage from Sunday Island to Lagoon Island (Bird Islands).

2 June

The day's work (from 6 a.m. to noon). Bligh here, when off a cape he wrongly believes is Cape York, corrects his DR longitude by comparing it to his position fifteen minutes of longitude east of the Cape. As explained elsewhere, Bligh was the victim of two errors in this matter.

3 June

The day's work divided into two sections, the first from noon 2 June (or start of 3 June) to Turtle Island, the second from the 5.30 a.m. departure from Turtle Island to noon position in Prince of Wales Channel. The two sets of northing and westing are added to give the total for the day. The bearing and distance of Timor are calculated; calculations of observed latitude.

4 June

The day's work; sextant and latitude calculations; bearing and distance of Timor.

5 June

The day's work, observed latitude calculations, bearing and distance of Timor.

6 June

The day's work, latitude calculations and bearing and distance of Timor.
The position being used for Timor in the daily calculations is a combination of
Hamilton Moore's latitude for its northern end (which was in fact about 30
minutes too far south) and the *Tables Requisite* longitude (which in fact was over
four and a half degrees too far east of the northern end of Timor).

7 June

The day's work; sextant and latitude calculations; bearing and distance of Timor.

Page 75a [7 June]

This page, although placed in the original between those for 2 and 3 June, contains rough calculations made early in the afternoon of Sunday 7 June (nautical date), together with a sketch map in pencil showing a number of islands, and with the words 'New Guinea' in one place. There is also writing along the left margin, including the legible phrase '… to stay in the Boat'. The calculations in ink at the top of the page are concerned with the bread supply and its duration

with a twice and a thrice daily issue. The figures further down the page and those
in an inverted position at the bottom left reflect Bligh's growing anxiety that he
might miss Timor altogether. The first set shows his DR position at noon on
7 June and the difference of longitude between the latter and the eastern point
of Timor as given in the *Tables Requisite*. The inverted figures show a position for
the southwestern tip of Timor, probably obtained by 'averaging' the figures given
in the *Tables Requisite* and Hamilton Moore, and an attempt to estimate the
latitude span of his target, Timor.

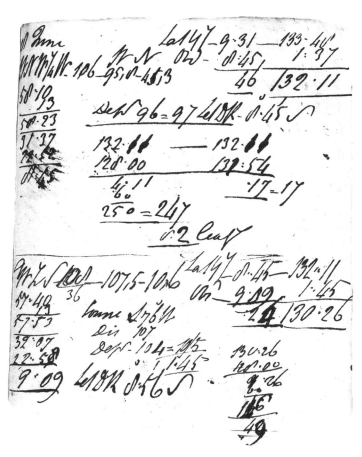

8 June

The day's work; sextant and latitude calculations; comparison of the difference
of longitudes given by alternative longitudes for Timor, resulting in the choice of
Hamilton Moore's figure to calculate the bearing and distance.

9 June

The day's work; sextant and latitude calculations; difference of longitude
to Timor.

10 June

The day's work; sextant and latitude calculations; bearing and distance of the eastern part of Timor.

11 June

The day's work; sextant and latitude calculations; expression of fear that the launch may be too far north and in danger of missing Timor. This fear was caused by the wrong position of 9°S latitude given by Hamilton Moore for the north end of Timor.

12 June

The day's work; sextant and latitude calculations. Timor was seen at 3 a.m. on this day and the launch placed on an offshore course until daylight, when a south-westerly course was assumed.

13 June

The day's work; no observation of sun, so southing is added to the previous latitude to give DR latitude. This is later amended to 10° 20'S by applying the 7'7" of northing made during the next twenty-four hours to the observed latitude of the next day to get retrospectively a more accurate figure for this day.

14 June

The day's work, ending at Kupang (Coupang). A note says the log has been completed up to Kupang.

BIBLIOGRAPHY

BACH, J. *William Bligh*. Melbourne, 1967.

BARNEY, S. Minutes of the Court Martial Held at Portsmouth August 12, 1790. In *The Australiana Facsimiles, Volume 11*. Melbourne, 1952.

BARROW, J. *The Eventful History of the Mutiny and Piratical Seizure of H.M.S. Bounty its Causes and Consequences*. London, 1831.

BEAGLEHOLE, J. C. *The Journals of Captain James Cook on His Voyages of Discovery*, vol. 1. Cambridge, 1955.

BLIGH, W. Log of His Majesty's Ship *Bounty*. Manuscript, 2 vols, Mitchell Library, Sydney.

————*Log of H.M.S.* Bounty, *1787-89*. London, 1975.

————*Log of H.M.S.* Providence, *1791-93*. London, 1976.

————*A Narrative of the Mutiny on board His Majesty's Ship Bounty; and the subsequent voyage of part of the crew, in the ship's boat, from Tofoa, one of the Friendly Islands, to Timor, a Dutch Settlement in the East Indies*. London, 1790.

————*A Voyage to the South Sea*. London, 1792.

———— *The Mutiny on Board H.M.S. Bounty 1789*. Guildford, 1981.

BOUGAINVILLE, L. A. de *A Voyage Round the World Performed by Order of His Most Christian Majesty, in the Years 1766, 1767, 1768 and 1769*. London, 1772.

BOWKER, R. M. *Mutiny! Aboard H.M. Armed Transport 'Bounty' in 1789*. Old Bosham, Sussex, 1978.

CHANDLER, J. E. *Beloved, Respected and Lamented*. Marlborough, 1979.

DANIELSSON, B. *What Happened on the* Bounty. London, 1963.

DARBY, M. *Who Caused the Mutiny on the* Bounty. Sydney, 1965.

DE RIETZ, R. (ED.) *Studia Bountyana*, vol. 1, Uppsala, 1965.

FORBES, E. *The Birth of Scientific Navigation*. London, 1974.

FRYER, J. Narrative, 1789. Manuscript. Mitchell Library, Sydney.

———— *The voyage of the* Bounty *launch*. Genesis Press facsimile, Guildford, England, and Rigby, Adelaide, 1979.

HENDERSON, G. C. *The Discoverers of the Fiji Islands*. London, 1933.

HOUGH, R. *Captain Bligh and Mr Christian*. London, 19172.

JOLLIFE, J. *East Timor, Nationalism and Colonialism*. Brisbane, 1978.

KEMP, P. (ED.) *The Oxford Companion to Ships and the Sea*. Oxford, 1979.

MACKANESS, G. *The Life of Vice-Admiral William Bligh*. Sydney, 1931.

MOORE, HAMILTON J. *The New Practical Navigator; Being a Complete Epitome of Navigation*. London, 1814.

MORRISON, J. Journal of H.M.S. *Bounty* and at Tahiti. Manuscript. Mitchell Library, Sydney.

————Memorandum and Particulars Respecting the *Bounty* and her Crew. Manuscript, Mitchell Library, Sydney

RUTTER, O. *Voyage of the* Bounty's *Launch as Related in William Bligh's Despatch to the Admiralty and the Journal of John Fryer*. London, 1934.

SHARP, A. *The Discovery of the Pacific Islands*. Oxford, 1960.

SHAW, A. G. L. 'William Bligh (1754-1817)', *Australian Dictionary of Biography*, Vol. 1. Melbourne, 1968.

SLATER, P. *A Field Guide to Australian Birds, Non-Passerines*. Adelaide, 1970.

TAYLOR, E. G. R. *The Haven Finding Art*. London, 1971.

_____ *Navigation in the Days of Captain Cook*. London, 1975.

The Admiralty Navigation Manual, 3 vols. London, 1938.

The Australian Encyclopaedia. Sydney, 1983.

Encyclopaedia Britannica. Chicago, 1967.

THE LIST OF MUTINEERS

                                        feet   In
Fletcher Christian. Aged 24 Years – 5 .. 9 High Dark Swarthy
                                                Complexion

Complexion ⎯⎯⎯⎯⎯ Dark & very swathy
Hair ⎯⎯⎯⎯⎯⎯⎯⎯ Blackish or very dark brown
Make ⎯⎯⎯⎯⎯⎯⎯⎯ Strong
Marks ⎯⎯⎯⎯⎯⎯⎯ Star tatowed on the left breast and
                        tatowed on the backside. – His knees
                        stands a little out and may be called a
                        little bow legged. He is subject to violent
                        perspiration & particularly in His hands
                        so that he soils anything he handles.

                            ft   In
George Stewart – aged 23 – 5 .. 7 – High –
Complexion ⎯⎯⎯⎯ Good
Hair ⎯⎯⎯⎯⎯⎯⎯⎯ Dark
Make ⎯⎯⎯⎯⎯⎯ Slender & narrow chested & long kneck
Marks ⎯⎯⎯⎯⎯⎯ Star on the left breast – one on the left arm –
tatowed on the backside – A Heart with darts on the left arm – Small face
& black Eyes.

                            f   in
Peter Haywood ⎯⎯⎯ Aged 17 – 5 .. 7
Complexion ⎯⎯⎯⎯ Fair
Hair ⎯⎯⎯⎯⎯⎯⎯⎯ Light brown
Make ⎯⎯⎯⎯⎯⎯⎯⎯ Well proportioned
Marks ⎯⎯⎯⎯⎯⎯⎯⎯⎯ Very much tattowed and on the Right
Leg is tattowed The Three legs of Man as that coin is. At this time he had
not done growing – He speaks with Strong Manks or I. of Man accent

                            ft   in
Edward Young ⎯⎯⎯ Aged 22 .. 5 .. 8 High
Complexion ⎯⎯⎯⎯⎯ Dark and rather a bad look
Hair ⎯⎯⎯⎯⎯⎯⎯⎯ Dark Brown
Make ⎯⎯⎯⎯⎯⎯ Strong
Marks ⎯⎯⎯⎯⎯⎯ Lost several of his fore teeth & those that
remain are all rotten. – A small mole on the left side of the throat and on
the right arm is tatowed a Heart & Dart through it with E .. Y underneath
and the date of the year 1788 or 1789

ft. In

Cha.⁵ Churchill. Aged 30 Years – 5 .. 10 High

Complexion _____ fair

Hair _____ Short light Brown. Top of the Head Bald

Make _____ Strong

Marks _____The Fore Finger of his left hand
Crooked and his hand shows the Marks of a Severe Scald. Tatowed in
several places of the Body, Legs and Arms –

James Morrison _____ Aged 28 Years – 5 .. 8

Complexion _____ Sallow

Hair _____ Long Black Hair

Make _____ Slender

Marks _____ Lost the Use of the Upper Joint of the Fore
Finger of the Right Hand – Tatowed with a Star under his left Breast &
a Garter round his Left leg with the Motto of Honi Soit Qui Mal y Pense
– has been wounded in One of his Arms with a Musquet Ball.

f   i

John Mills _____ Aged 40 Years _____ 5 .. 10

Complexion _____ fair

Hair _____ Light Brown

Make _____ Strong. Raw Boned.

Marks _____ Scar in his Right Arm Pit –

ft   In

John Millward _____ Aged 22 years _____ 5 – 5 High

Complexion _____ Brown

Hair _____ Dark

Make _____ Strong

Marks _____ Very much Tatowed in Diff.ᵗ parts and is
marked the Pit of the Stomach with a Taoomy or Breastplate of
Otaheite –

ft. In

Matt.^w Thompson. Aged 40 Years _____ 5 .. 8
Complexion _____ Very Dark
Hair _____ Short Black
Make _____ Slender.
Marks _____ Lost the Joint of the Great Toe of his Right
foot – and is Tatowed in several places –

Wm Mickoy   . Aged 25 years – 5 .. 6 High
Complexion _____ Fair
Hair _____ Light Brown
Make _____ Strong
Marks _____ A Scar where he has been Stabbed in
the Belly – and a Small Scar under his Chin – is Tatowed.

Matt.^t Quintal ... Aged 21 years 5 .5
Complexion _____ Fair
Make _____ Strong
Marks _____ Very much tatowed on the Backside & several other
places
Legs & Arms

ft In

John Sumner _____ Aged 24 years – 5..8 – High
Complexion _____ Fair
Hair _____ Brown
Make _____ Slender
Marks _____ A Scar upon the left Cheek & tatowed
in several places

Thos Burkitt _____ Aged 26 years – 5..9 High
Complexion _____ fair very much pitted with the Small Pox
Hair _____ Brown
Make _____ Slender
Marks _____ Very much tatowed.

ft In

Isaac Martin .. Aged 30 Years 5 .. 11 High
Complexion _____ Sallow
Hair _____ Short Brown
Make _____ Raw Boned
Marks _____ Star on the left Breast –

                                              ft In
Wᵐ Muspratt _____ Aged 30 Years – 5.. 6 High
Complexion _____ Dark
Hair _____ Brown
Make _____ Slender
Marks _____ A very Strong Black Beard. Scars under
his Chin Tatowed

                                          ft In
Henʸ Hilbrant _____ Aged 25 Years 5 .. 7 High
Complexion _____ fair
Hair _____ Sandy
Make _____ Strong.
Marks _____ His Left Arm Shorter than the other having
been broke – is a Hanoverian Born & Speaks Bad English

                                              ft In
Alexʳ Smith _____ Aged 22 years 5.. 5 High
Complexion _____ Brown
Hair _____ Brown
Make _____ Strong
Marks _____ Very much pitted with the Small
[Pox] & very much tatowed on his Body, Legs, Arms & feet – & a Scar
on his Right foot where he has been cut with a Wood Ax

                                              ft In
John Williams _____ Aged 25 Years 5..5 High
Complexion _____ Dark
Hair _____ Black
Make _____ Slender
Marks   has a Scar on the back part of the Head and is a native of
Guernsey & Speaks French.

                                              ft. In
Richᵈ Skinner _____ Aged 22 Years 5-8 High
Complexion _____ Fair
Hair _____ Light Brown
Make _____ Well made
Marks _____ Scars on both Ankles & on his Right
Shin Very much tatowed by Trade a Hair Dresser.

ft In

Mich.! Byrn –   Aged 28 years 5 .. 6 High

Complexion _____ Fair

Hair _____ Short fair

Make _____ Slender

Marks _____ Almost Blind has the Marks of an Issue in the Back of his Neck

ft In

Tho.ˢ Ellison _____ Aged 17 years _____ 5 ..3

Complexion _____ fair

Hair _____ Dark

Make _____ Strong

Marks _____ Has got his Name tatowed on his Right Arm. and dated Oct.ʳ 25.ᵗʰ 1788 –

ft In

Wᵐ. Brown _____ Aged 27 Years _____ 5..8 High

Complexion _____ Fair

Hair _____ Dark Brown

Make _____ Slender

Marks _____ A remarkable Scar on one of his Cheeks Which contracts the Eye Lid and runs down to his throat Occasioned by the Kings Evil – is Tatowed –

f   i

Jos.ʰ Coleman Armourer _____ Aged 40 Years _____ 5..6

Complexion _____ fair

Hair _____ Grey.

Make _____ Strong

Marks _____ A Heart Tatowed on One of his Arms and 5777 –

ft In

Tho.ˢ M.ᶜIntosh – Carp.ˢ Mate – Aged 28 years _____ 5..6

Complexion _____ Fair

Hair _____ Light Brown

Make _____ Slender

Marks _____ pitted with the Small Pox

ft In

Cha.ˢ Norman Carp.ˢ Mate – 26 Years _____ 5.. 9

Complexion _____ fair

Hair _____ Light Brown

Make _____ Slender

Marks _____ pitted with the Small Pox has a

Remarkable Motion with his head and eyes_____

Turn Over

These – Joseph Coleman – Mich.ˡ Byrne – Tho.ˢ McIntosh and Cha.ˢ Norman are deserving of mercy being detained against their inclinations. –

Wm Bligh